THE TECHNIQUES OF SOFT TOYMAKING

By the same author:

The Great Soft Toy Cat & Kitten Book (1981)

Crafts & the Disabled (1982)

The Techniques of Soft Toymaking

ENID ANDERSON

B T Batsford Ltd, London

This book is dedicated to
B. M. H. – Godmother and friend

ACKNOWLEDGEMENTS

My sincere thanks to Pauline Stride, who was the craft editor with B. T. Batsford when this book was accepted for publication, for all her interest at that time. Iris Dwyer who typed the manuscript. Ray Banks, of Windsor Spice Studios, who so patiently photographs all my samples. June Arnold who always enjoys our craftwork and gives me much help. My family have given me extensive support during the putting together of the manuscript; without their help my craft ventures would be an impossibility.

I was motivated at the start of my craft career by many people, but possibly mainly by the books I read on the various craft subjects. I should like to give a special mention to the work of the late Margaret Hutchings, whose books taught me many facts on the subject of toymaking, and to Baroness de Sarigny's work, particularly her book *Good Design in Soft Toys*.

First published 1982
© Enid Anderson 1982

Reprinted 1983

ISBN 0 7134 2391 9

Printed in Great Britain
by The Pitman Press Ltd
Bath Avon
for the publishers,
B T Batsford Ltd,
4 Fitzhardinge Street, London, W1H 0AH

Contents

Acknowledgements
Introduction

PART I General principles of toymaking

1. Development of soft toymaking in relation to other types
   of toys   *8*
2. Tools and materials   *12*
3. Understanding patterns   *16*
4. Basic techniques   *19*
5. Designing soft toys   *42*
6. Processes which may provide a useful extension to soft toy
   techniques   *60*
7. Features and characteristics   *69*
8. Finishing a toy   *92*

PART II Techniques related to specific toy types

9. Jack-in-the-box   *108*
10. Jack-in-the-box puppet   *113*
11. Knitted toys   *114*
12. Flat toys made from the stitch-around method   *116*
13. Glove puppetry   *117*

PART III Adapting toys with a historical connection to soft
toymaking

14. The Marotte   *124*
15. Two-faced dolls   *125*
16. Double-ended dolls   *128*
17. Pantin or jumping jack   *129*

PART IV Professional toymaking

18. Getting your toy designs published   *134*
19. Making toys commercially   *135*
20. Showing and exhibiting toys   *137*

Bibliography   *140*
List of craft suppliers   *141*
Index   *143*

Introduction

This book crept up on me. I had very little time for writing owing to my craft commitments, but then due to an illness which affected my sight I had an enforced three months of rest with plenty of time to sit and think. The idea of a book on soft toy techniques began to take shape in my mind. When I commenced my work again I was so busy all thoughts of a book were impossible. Then my students repeatedly said they wished I would write down my ideas, so that they had a reference book to consult when they were not in the classroom. I decided then that if I was to add yet another craft book to the market, it must be entirely different from previous editions on the subject, and cover as many aspects of soft toy-making as possible, and therefore hopefully be useful to a much wider audience.

Of all the craft subjects I teach, soft toymaking is the one that students have usually attempted at one time or the other, and because so many patterns appear regularly in women's magazines the students often have examples of their finished work. Especially in the more mature student one encounters a definite blockage: 'I can make soft toys.' It is interesting to note how many of these students come up to me after the lesson and admit: 'I never realised there was so much to learn.'

I sincerely hope this book will help toymakers to put the professional touch to their toys, introduce soft toymaking to those of you who may not have attempted the subject and perhaps add some processes to the repertoire of the professional toymaker. It is the most relaxing and creative therapy.

A soft toy can be simple in design, need not be expensive to make, but will be a definite favourite of the recipient.

Possibly the best advice a craft tutor can give students is, enjoy your craftwork; this will be reflected in the finished article. Learn to look and see all around you; details observed can make all the difference to the finish of the toy. Knowledge of the materials you are using will enable you to create and achieve the maximum from them.

It was difficult to know where to draw the line between true soft toymaking and other processes which partly involve soft toymaking. I have therefore used the criterion and licence of including some examples and techniques which deviate from the true definition of soft toymaking, hoping that the inclusion of these may assist you in enhancing your soft toys and provide other avenues of interest to pursue such as, for example, puppetry.

It would have been nice to have had unrestricted space to set down an exhaustive list of techniques; however, I do hope that by the end of this book you will have added to your knowledge of soft toymaking and that you will derive much enjoyment and satisfaction from creating your own toy subjects.

I am at present working on a manuscript on *Applying Soft Toy Techniques* as a follow up which will include many toy patterns related to the techniques in this book; this will enable the toymakers who may not wish to design their own toy patterns to apply the knowledge gained in this book using my toy designs, and the wide range of patterns will also be useful to the established toymakers.

Part 1
General principles of toymaking

1 Development of soft toymaking in relation to other types of toys

From the earliest times children have been amused by all types of toys. Children played with dried fruit and because of the seeds in them they became rattles. Cave children played with balls made from animal bladders, and bundles of rags and furs became dolls. Whilst soft dolls are still very popular today, they can be traced back in history, although they first appeared more as religious or fertility symbols than playthings. The British Museum has a rag doll from Roman times which was found in a child's grave dating back to 300 BC. Hull Museum has a toy clay boat complete with oarsmen which was made in the Bronze Age approximately 4000 years ago. Ancient Egyptians made clay dolls with arms and legs which could be moved, and their children also played with balls made of plaited papyrus. So often toys developed from weapons, or from articles used in the past for a completely different reason than amusement. An example of this is the yo-yo, which was used in the Far East as a weapon. Kites helped the Chinese 2000 years ago to measure distance.

Some toys were used in ancient times as a means of training the children in adult activites; boys had miniature bows and arrows, the girls spindles.

Even in ancient times the people were health conscious. Greek toys, for example the hoop, were designed to encourage the children to exercise. The game of five stones is used by children today, which has its origin in Greek times.

In Roman times girls had jointed toys and small clay cups and plates. Also made in clay were rattles in the shape of pigs and birds. In 1391 the Queen of England had a set of dolls sent from France to show her the fashions being worn in the French Court. This idea became a normal occurrence until well into the eighteenth century, so that the ladies' own dressmakers could make the fashions. These dolls were given to the daughters of the household after their mothers had viewed them.

The hobby horse was possibly introduced into Britain by the Normans. In the fourteenth century small boys carried a kind of whirring windmill which they used as a toy jousting lance and which was intended to knock their opponents off their hobby horses.

Many toy types have not survived the ravages of time. At the beginning of the middle ages toys were made from paper, rags, wood and clay, including soldiers, dolls and furniture. These were sold at markets and fairs; for example, at St Bartholomew's Day Fair, held in London each year for hundreds of years from the twelfth century on the 24th August. The word 'doll' was not used in England until the end of the seventeenth century. Before then they were called 'babes' or 'babies' or 'toy babies'. 'Bartholomew babies' were dolls bought at the great fair.

The fourteenth century saw an advancement in popularity of puppet shows, including Punch and Judy. The sixteenth and seventeenth centuries saw a progress in making toys which spread all over the world.

DOLLS

There are very few soft dolls of any considerable age available. Rag dolls were intended to be played with; this was the reason for their unbreakable structure. They were obviously less expensive than more elaborate dolls. These can be seen in museums, made of wax, bisque or composition materials, and due to their delicate construction they were mainly used as showpieces and not played with.

Early dolls were often made of wood and leather and stuffed with bran. Cheaper versions were made of cloth and were often hollow for filling with coins and sweets as gifts. German dolls had movable arms and legs. Simple Dutch dolls had painted hair and jointed arms and legs; these were very popular and were called 'Flanders babies' or 'Penny woods'. Franklin Darrow of Bristol, Connecticut, applied for a patent in 1865 for rawhide dolls (dolls made of leather before it was tanned). The dolls' heads were made by pouring the bran into the required shape and attaching it to a stuffed body.

FRENCH DOLLS

The nineteenth century was the age of many beautiful dolls. One of the most famous dollmakers was Jumeau, who had a factory in Paris. The dolls' bodies were made of the softest leather, and had beautiful wax modelled heads. The eyes were in glass and each hair and eyelash was applied separately. These dolls were expensive; even in 1882 they cost as much as £5. As early as 1880 some could actually talk. Not only were rag dolls available at that time but also soft animals.

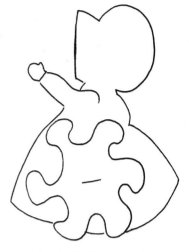

DIAGRAM 1 Walking paper doll

Early in the twentieth century dolls were mainly aimed at the adult market and often called 'boudoir' or 'art' dolls.

Large numbers of dolls were bought in 1871. A London factory was at that time producing 20,000 wax dolls each week.

In 1874 the United States issued a patent to W. H. Hart Jnr. for a walking paper doll. Many firms have over the past years produced mechanical walking dolls of a more complex nature.

The original walking paper dolls had anywhere from four to six feet on the wheel. Some of the dolls had the front printed only and the rotating wheel fixed on the reverse side. Other dolls had both front and back views and the wheels were inserted in the middle of the two-piece doll. The latter versions had a small hole or slot through which a piece of dowelling could be inserted and this made the walking movement of the doll easier. The wheels required careful application so that only two of the feet appeared below the skirt at one time.

Fraulein Margarete Steiff and Frau Kathe Kruse are two women who established famous manufacturing concerns. Margarete Steiff (1847–1909) was a polio victim who made stuffed animals as a hobby; eventually, due to much interest being shown in her toys, she formed a small business. By 1900 she was exporting all over the world. Later she added jointed dolls to her repertoire. In 1912 Kathe Kruse started making beautiful cloth dolls with metal reinforced faces.

Beatrix Potter, authoress of *Peter Rabbit* and other books, tried in 1889 to interest factories in England to produce soft toys; however, she was not successful as the London toy factories were not willing to compete against the cheap German toys.

In the early 1890s a very popular type of soft doll was the cut out fabric doll. This was printed on a calico material, with the front and back of the toy illustrated ready to cut out and stitch round the outside edge, turned to the right side and stuffed. These were amongst the first two-piece dolls. In the *Girl's Own* paper dated 1894 instructions were given for making a soft doll out of flesh coloured suede for the face and pink sateen for the body. Two English firms, Samuel Finburgh and Co. and Deans Rag Book Co. Ltd, produced thousands of cut-out rag toys; then the Dean's Rag Book Co. realised the value of a book which could not be torn apart and the rag book was designed. They also produced printed cut out doll sheets which they described as 'knock about' toys. Today we see a revival of the printed sheet toys based on the same principal as the earlier designs, but they have progressed considerably. For example, there is a Noah's ark with animals to fit into the ark, or a dachshund dog with a zip fastener in its under gusset into which puppies fit; there are many attractive designs.

TEDDY BEARS

The teddy bear appeared in the toy world in about 1903. Its origin is often attributed to being American; however, it is interesting to note that the German Company of Frau Margarete Steiff accepted an order from America at the Leipzig Fair in 1903 for 3000 bears a year to be exported to America.

The bear originated from a bear cub in a cartoon by Clifford Berryman which showed Teddy Roosevelt after a hunt in the Rocky Mountains, with a small brown cub in the background. This inspired Morris Michtom to produce a toy bear in plush, in a small shop in Brooklyn. At first his wife helped sew the toys. It grew very quickly in popularity and out of this small beginning the Ideal Toy corporation of America was formed. The teddy bear is possibly the most successful toy figure of all, and whilst he has retained his basic shape over generations, certain characteristics have changed with fashion and advanced technology, for example, better quality fur fabrics and a wider range of colours. The modern teddy bear has a shorter snout than the original versions.

THE GOLLIWOG

This was created in 1895 by Florence Upton in her book *The Adventures of Two Dutch Dolls and a Golliwog*. The earlier golliwogs had protruding noses and were more frightening than the more modern versions. Traditionally they wear a uniform consisting of a blue jacket, a waistcoat and striped trousers usually coloured red and white. Messrs Dean introduced a white faced Golliwog and named him 'Mr Smith'. The Golliwog was extremely popular for many years, his woolly hair and later image of a wide grinning smile captivated very young children. Unfortunately due to changing social attitudes he is not so in fashion now.

MORE RECENT TYPES

In 1912 the Kewpie all-bisque baby dolls became fashionable. They were designed in the United States by Rose O'Neil.

During the 1914—18 war many women made soft toys. The cinema in the 1930s had a positive effect on toy production. Characters, for example Mickey Mouse, Shirley Temple and Charlie Chaplin, all became popular toys. Film-making created a natural start to the progression of animated characters into soft toy form.

Over the years further versions of the old favourites have occurred. The teddy bear changed species and became a panda, linked to a zoo birth. Societies adopted soft toys as their mascots, and the World Wildlife Fund adopted the panda.

Television made its mark on the toy world, especially in the puppetry field. Viewers have learned the vast potential of puppets because the television media covers not only the intricate puppet types but also the simplest forms of puppet characters. The literary world, for example, with Pooh bear, Rupert bear and Paddington bear, Disney characters and, more recently, Snoopy, the Wombles and the Muppets have all made their impression on the soft toy market. It is necessary for manufacturers to purchase the right to produce characters from a film, book or television. Companies who control copyright of character design do a big business with spin-offs into related commercial fields.

Children are most receptive to soft toys between the ages of six months to eight years, often longer depending on the individual. Teenage girls often retain an interest into adulthood showing a liking for cuddly ornamental toys (for example, giant teddy bears). Boys tend to lose interest in soft toys about the age of six; again, the age varies. Boys later use soft toys as mascots for football teams, and universities often use large soft toys as mascots. Often miniature soft toys can be seen in cars as hanging ornaments. It is a common sight to see a battered soft toy wired to the front of workmen's lorries or refuse lorries. Soft toys also enter the world of adults in the shape of cushions, snake draught excluders, etc.

During the late '50s revolutionary American artists such as Roy Lichtenstein constructed gigantic hamburgers, telephones, typewriters, televisions etc. from fabric and stuffing (also in vinyls and moulded and melted plastics), the concept being to cause unease or mild shock in the beholder seeing a familiar, sophisticated object rendered in an unfamiliar medium and texture in a toy-like way — an expression of irreverence for contemporary society and the art forms of the past. This trend was followed by 'souvenir' and home ornament manufacturers, who mass produced in small fabrics telephones, televisions, dice, and plates of food as 'fun' decoration for the home.

SAFETY AND DESIGN

With the advance of time we have seen the regulating of safety factors in relation to soft toymaking. In the earlier days toy eyes were often pulled off then swallowed, and the lead in the paint used was toxic to children, whose first action is always to put the toy in the mouth. Wiring was dangerous, fillings often inflammable. With the aid of laws and the work of the Design Council many problems have now been eradicated.

A useful leaflet which is available from Her Majesty's Stationery Office is the Statutory Instrument No. 1367, *Consumer Protection: The Toys (Safety) Regulations 1974*. This lists safety regulations for various toy types; certain items, however, are specifically for soft toys. If you are going to be making soft toys in a serious way you would do well also to keep *au fait* with the latest British Standards publications (e.g. B.S. 3443 and 5665) and the European Standards (E.N. 71), where agreed guidelines are still being formulated.

2 Tools and materials

The tools for toymaking are not expensive and are readily available from large stores, haberdashers, stationers, D.I.Y. shops, hardware stores, etc. For specific toymaking items — for example, musical units, bells, eyes, etc. — it is necessary to contact a specialist retail outlet, and mail order firms which are able to service orders on an international scale are listed at the back of the book. Most firms offer more attractive terms for bulk orders so it is well worth the effort of contacting other toymakers in the area who may be willing to share in the material order. The quantity of equipment and materials will naturally vary according to the amount of toymaking done. For someone who occasionally makes a soft toy it is possible to improvise and use the basic items from a normal workbox; on the other hand, if a great deal of toymaking is undertaken, it is of benefit gradually to build up the amount of equipment. Once the list of stock is completed, do make sure this equipment is well looked after, especially the cutting out scissors, which should be carefully kept for that specific purpose.

Another point to consider is the safety factor; never leave pins and sewing needles stuck into any surface except a pin cushion. Even if you are fortunate in having a room whose main function is as a sewing room, do tidy up and clean away after work. If a muddle continually exists the situation will not resolve itself and the result could well be badly made toys, possibly even dangerous ones if the pins are not removed.

For storing, plastic tool boxes are available with sections of various sizes, which are ideal for the smaller items of equipment. These tool boxes are usually stocked in D.I.Y. stores and are inexpensive to purchase. Haberdashery-type stores stock expanding wooden workboxes which are also excellent for keeping the smaller sewing items.

Scissors store well if placed in material bags with an outside plastic covering; this avoids any dampness which could produce a poor performance. The following is a list of tools necessary for most soft toymaking requirements.

WORKBOX TOOLS

Sharp pointed scissors (a length of 20.4cm (8in) is useful)

Thin round-nosed pliers (for jointing toys)

Sewing needles of assorted sizes and thicknesses, including a curved needle

Wire brush for raising the pile on fur fabric toys

Packet pins: ordinary pins, long dressmaker's pins, and pins with coloured heads (it is essential that they are rustproof so that they do not mark the fabric)

Hammer (preferably about 2.5cm (1in) diameter on the hammering face)

Wire cutters (or tin snips)

Pair of compasses for making circles

Drawing pins (thumb tacks)

Set square

Box of drawing pins of assorted sizes for use in cutting felt circles for eyes

Leather punch — ideal for punching out felt circles for toy eyes

Sewing thread. Synthetic thread (such as Sylko), terylene thread, in colours which match the fabrics, and button thread

Embroidery stranded yarn (such as Anchor) in a variety of colours

Graph paper, squared, preferably 2.5cm (1in) grid

Thin card for mounting patterns (e.g. cereal packets)

Tracing paper or greaseproof paper

All-purpose adhesive (such as Copydex or Elmer's Glue-All) for materials and card etc.

Adhesive tape

Office folders, 35.5cm x 22.9cm (14in x 9in), for storing patterns on a shelf or in a cardboard box

MATERIALS FOR SPECIAL PURPOSES

(Various fabrics are discussed in the next section)

Stuffing: kapok, soft stuffing and washable filling (other stuffings are discussed in Ch. 4)

Stuffing sticks of various sizes: dowelling, wooden knitting needles or thick cane, with a V-shaped notch cut in the end to grip the filling, wooden meat skewers, wooden cocktail sticks, handles of wooden spoons, etc.

Pipe cleaners (for stiffening ears etc.), electrical wire, galvanised wire (for wiring toys), florist's wire — all these have their uses in stiffening and support processes.

Electrical tape, ordinary tape or strips of sheeting to cover wires

Joint sets in various sizes. Wooden or hardboard discs are preferable; avoid plastic discs because they are not really satisfactory in long term use

Musical units: growlers, squeakers, bells, tinklers and musical movements

Safety lock eyes of various types and sizes. A tool for applying these eyes, which has four ferrules of different sizes. Foam pads to act as a pad whilst hammering eyes into place

Screwdriver and pliers to remove metal eye backs which have been inserted in the wrong place

GLUES SUITABLE FOR MODEL AND SOFT TOYMAKING

1. Araldite for hard surfaces
2. PVA water-soluble resin glue for mask making (also excellent for adding wigs to models, as it dries clear)
3. Copydex for applying felt features, as it is absorbed into all surfaces of the felt. (Many glue types only glue the surface 'hairs' or fibres of the felt together so that they can easily be plucked off the toy by tiny fingers and the toy spoilt)
4. UHU, Bostick No. 1, JOY all-pupose glues are excellent for paper construction

FABRICS

We live in an age when the materials available for toymakers give endless opportunities. Sometimes the fabric design alone 'makes' the toy, with very little effort on the part of the toymaker. A brown print design may suggest a hen, a zigzag design may suggest a snake, while tiny print designs are excellent for making small creatures such as mice. If the material does not immediately suggest a toy subject, lay it out for a while and the answer will come. Even when using materials from a scrap bag, do not be caught in the trap of thinking that anything will do; it is far more professional to design a toy around the material — one that complements it.

Until a comparatively short time ago fabrics were often categorised into accepted materials for particular types of toys. At one time pastel-coloured soft toys were the vogue, then teddy bears became the favourites, usually in traditional golden tones and synthetic fur fabrics. Then an assortment of dogs, rabbits and other animals abounded, all in a given set of colours. Now things are much more exciting; the toymaker can look through books and magazines to find an endless range of animal and other subjects, and depict them in bright colours and fancy patterns which need not be faithful to the natural colouring of the animal. Today we find it acceptable to cover a giraffe shape with a flowered cotton print, for example, rather than realistic brown patches — this is a matter of taste and fashion rather than correctness.

In fact, most materials are suitable for toymaking, although it is wise to avoid the thin, slippery fabrics for toy 'skins', as they are more difficult to work and not so pleasant to hold. Felts, leather, velvet, heavy curtain material, Courtelle fleece, flannelette, cotton, tweed, and many more types can all be used. Toys may also be knitted using woollen or synthetic yarns, and the knitted sections joined and stuffed in the usual way. When buying a fabric always check if it is washable, as soft toys become dirty during play and often need to be cleaned. Soft toys made from towelling make excellent bathtoys when filled with a quick-drying stuffing such as foam chips. All washed toys should of course be thoroughly dried before being returned to the child for play. If the fabric is not washable, ask the sales assistant how it should be cleaned. Not all toys, puppets and ornamental models, for example, will require washing or cleaning, so for these purposes the appearance of the fabric is more important than its durability. Generally speaking, synthetic fabrics are easier to clean than natural ones (such as cotton and wool), because the dirt tends to lie on the surface rather than work its way between the fibres.

Certain fabrics are unsuitable for very young children; for example, shaggy, acrylic pile fur fabric. In fact in some instances certain long pile fabrics can be dangerous; if a child has a tendency to an asthmatic condition this fabric could aggravate the condition. As a general rule, close-pile synthetic fur fabrics are the most useful for babies' toys, as they are fully washable; the longer pile fabrics are more suitable for the older child.

To make toys at very little cost either use scraps left from previously bought fabrics kept in a rag bag, or look around your home area for any textile manufacturers or distributors. So often large quantities of dress materials or curtain materials are thrown away by large firms. In some cases the size of material pieces may be small but it is possible to use ones ingenuity to design a toy around the material to hand. Local markets will sometimes sell a bundle of remnants which are of no use to them and will only charge a small amount. Look out during the sales for oddments of trimmings and curtain sample books, or ask at the local shops for outdated pattern books.

Fur fabrics
So often a poor quality fur fabric can waste hours of sewing time and bring great disappointment to the toymaker. There are some very poor synthetic fur fabrics available; the best way to avoid buying these is to do the following test. Run the thumb and first finger against the pile of the fabric. If it is thick and springy then it should make up well; if the pile is sparse and limp it will be impossible to hide the seams in the finished toy, or stop the pile parting at ear and tail edges. It is not always the most inexpensive fur fabric that is poor in this way; sometimes an expensive one can have the same faults. The one exception to this is very smooth, slightly shiny pile fur fabric called polished, the type which may be suitable for making a seal or a smooth coated animal. To test its quality, see how the pile lays on the backing cloth; if it is well covered in spite of being smooth it should be satisfactory in use.

It is not economical to buy the smallest amount of material such as a quarter yard or a quarter metre; it is much more useful and cheaper to buy a minimum of half a yard or half a metre. Fur fabrics are usually sold in 122–137cm (48–54in) widths. It is rare in ordinary toymaking to use real fur; the price is restrictive and real skins are mainly used for actual model toys and cannot be washed.

Knitted and stretchy fabrics

Stockinette is an excellent material for making a soft doll's body, especially when needle-modelling is required. It can be moulded to achieve whatever character is required. If you cannot obtain the skin tone you require it is an easy task to dip the fabric in tea to dye it (approximately one tea bag to 1 litre (2 pints) of water.

Felt

Felt is not a woven material; it consists of fibres matted under pressure — therefore it has no warp or weft. Felt varies considerably in quality and a good quality felt should be used for most toymaking. Avoid 'slipper' felts as these are much too thick for toymaking. As a general guide to quality, hold the felt up to the light and make sure it does not show thick and thin areas. Felt is available in a wide range of colours and as it does not fray it is an excellent medium for building up a toy such as a dragon or parrot which may require tone variations.

Leather

When using leather for toymaking be very careful to get the stretch of the animal's skin in the right direction. Leathers suitable for making gloves are sometimes suitable for toymaking, especially if they are supple. Leathers are most useful for trimming — harnesses, noses, hooves, etc.

Velvet and velveteen

Whilst velvets have a range of uses in soft toymaking with subjects such as pigs or other animals which require a short, close pile surface, it is not the easiest of fabrics to work with.

Soft furnishings

These are useful in toymaking, especially for stylised toys. They have bold designs which, if carefully considered at the design stage of your toy, can be selected and used to advantage. Some soft furnishing materials tend to be rather coarse and heavy and these are best avoided.

PAPER AND CARD

You will need good quality drawing paper for your finished toy designs; tracing paper; office-type folders for storage of patterns in a file; large hardback folders and lined paper for note taking; strong card for transferring finished designs; newspaper or brown paper for the original pattern cutting.

Men's paper tissue handkerchiefs are very useful for measuring a dolls size when designing and fitting clothes.

Materials required for papier mâché are described in Ch. 6.

STORING PATTERNS

There are various methods of storing patterns. The simplest is to use an office folder for each toy subject with the label clearly marked (for example, Rag Dolls, or Elephants) and to place these in alphabetical order in a cardboard box, adding new boxes as required. Within the folder the individual pattern and instructions should be kept in a clear plastic bag, with notes on the different colours and fabrics which have been used successfully on previous examples.

Another method is to make a hole in each pattern piece and fix it together by a pipe cleaner passed through the hole and twisted. Cord or tape can also be used in this way. Patterns may also be pegged together with plastic pegs.

3 Understanding patterns

Most bought patterns are ready to cut out and are the actual size of the toy to be made. In magazines they are often in a much smaller scale and need to be enlarged. Usually a reduced size pattern in a magazine states the grid size of graph paper to be used for increasing it to the actual size. The pattern is then simply drawn by hand onto the larger squares of the graph paper, following each line exactly from square to square; all that is required is meticulous care at this stage, just completing a portion at a time – the care will be reflected in a perfectly fitted toy.

On most patterns an arrow is marked to indicate the direction of the pile if the toy is to be made in fur fabric; otherwise it indicates the grain of the fabric. Commercial patterns state how many pieces to cut out of each pattern shape. It is often preferable to cut out each piece of fabric individually, mainly because some materials, even when pinned, tend to move, and this wastes material. Secondly, unless the material is very thin, one obtains a more accurate cut if cutting through a single thickness.

On a bought pattern the stitching line will be marked; be wary, however, as many instructions require a seam allowance of 0.7cm (¼in) or 1.3cm (½in) to be added to the basic pattern, while others already have the seam allowance included in the design. The phrase '0.7cm (or ¼in) seam allowance' means that the designer has already added on sufficient depth to the whole outline to allow a seam all round, so when cutting the toy out, cut on the given outline. If a pattern states 'no seam allowance', the outline given will be the stitching line and not the cutting line, so the fabric must be cut out at least 0.7cm (¼in) away from the outline, and it is preferable to measure this accurately all round and mark it with chalk before cutting. Some toys, particularly those made from Courtelle fleece, can be stitched all round the outline on a sewing machine, and cut out afterwards.

A beginner should not start with detailed patterns, as this could prove too difficult. It is much better to choose toys with perhaps two or three pieces so that full enjoyment in making them can be derived before moving on to more complicated projects. The trend in soft toys at the present time is to use very basic shapes and few features, so toys do not suffer in any way for their simplicity.

Coloured pins are essential for pinning the pattern to the fabric, as it is difficult to see dressmaker's pins against the paper and all too easy to tear the pattern when taking it off afterwards if one rogue pin has not been removed. Pins should be checked in number at the beginning of making and at the end, to ensure that none are left lying around as a safety hazard. If pins are not acceptable to the worker, small coloured plastic pegs can be obtained to hold fabric edges together before tacking or sewing.

TEMPLATES

Some tissue patterns are so frail that the pattern would only last a short while before tearing, and could not be used again and again unless they were first mounted onto card. Most patterns wear better in use if first pasted onto thin card, and this also makes it possible to obtain a more accurate outline when drawing round it onto the fabric. If a commercial pattern has many instructions written in different languages, underline in red the instructions written in English, or whatever your language is, so that a quick glance is all that is required to read the instructions on each piece.

Once mounted on card, the pattern can be used as a template to cut out large quantities of patterns if required, or can be passed from one person to another without fear of the pattern deteriorating. One point to add: when tracing a pattern from one which has been mounted on cardboard the new outline tends to become larger. One often finds after a number of subsequent tracings have been made that not only has the toy become appreciably larger but also — in extreme cases — the original amount of material quoted is no longer sufficient for the toy!

INSTRUCTIONS ON PATTERNS

Many mistakes can be avoided if all instructions (for example, pile line arrows, name of toy, part of toy, number of pieces, material to be used) are marked onto the patterns when tracing or designing them. It is a good policy to mark on the reverse side of the pattern those pieces which require to be reversed, or to have a second copy of the pattern piece cut out and marked in the reverse position.

ENLARGING AND REDUCING A PATTERN

Method 1

Many books and magazines have their toy patterns produced on a small scale, set on squares. It is then necessary to enlarge the pattern pieces to their correct size by enlarging onto graph paper. Usually the small pattern states, for example, 'each square represents 2.5cm (1in)', therefore it is necessary to either purchase some 2.5cm (1in) graph paper to enlarge onto or draw on plain paper 2.5cm (1in) squares. Accuracy in drawing your squares is essential. The size of the paper is determined by the number of squares on the small graph layout. When enlarging the design a great deal it helps to number the squares down one side and letter the squares across the top. Also number and letter the corresponding squares on the small layout. Re-draw the pattern pieces onto the enlarged sheet, using your lettering and numbering to assist in re-drawing accurately; care at this stage will result in an exact copy. Some people find it assists them if they add dots where the lines of the pattern cross the lines on the squared paper and then carefully draw and connect between the dots. To reduce a large pattern to a smaller size simply reverse the above process.

If the toy design is not already marked onto a graph, trace the design to be enlarged or reduced, then mark over the design in squares 0.7cm (¼in) or 1.3cm (½in) for small designs and 2.5cm (1in) for large, depending on the size of the design. Then on paper mark large squares — for

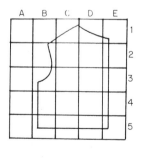

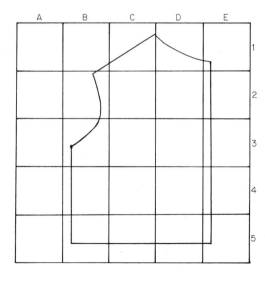

DIAGRAM 2 Enlarging a pattern.
Method 1

17

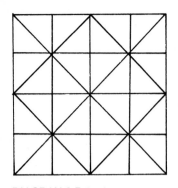

DIAGRAM 3 Enlarging a pattern.
Method 2

example to enlarge a design to twice the original size make the squares twice as large. Copy the design as already described.

Method 2

For very detailed toy patterns the layout with the extra diagonal lines assists in copying exact details.

Trace the design. Draw a frame around it. Draw a larger frame to the same proportions to fit the desired enlarged size. Draw diagonals corner to corner in each frame; where the diagonals meet is the centre point. To divide equally draw horizontal and vertical lines. Copy the design from the small version to the large one.

Method 3

Lay a ruler diagonally along AB; extend beyond B. Extend line AC. If you require the enlarged size to measure 30.5cm (12in) continue to extend lines AB and AC until a line drawn between D and E measures 30.5cm (12in). This is easily measured by holding a ruler vertically and sliding it across from the line BC until it registers 30.5cm (12in) between the line DE. Complete the outside lines of the enlarged square, rectangle, or whatever shape is being enlarged. Divide this larger square into the same number of small squares as the original one and then proceed to draw the pattern outline, carefully copying the exact portion contained in each of the original small squares. To reduce a pattern measure up the side BC of the original square to the height which the reduced toy is to be made; from this point draw a line parallel to top line FB of the square as far as the diagonal. From here draw a line parallel to BC down to AC to complete the new square, which is then divided into the same number of squares as the original one.

DIAGRAM 4 Enlarging and reducing a pattern. Method 3

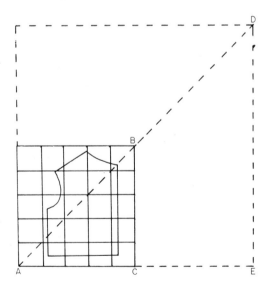
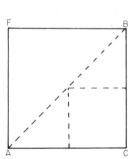

4 Basic techniques

MARKING OUT

Always mark out clearly and closely to the pattern templates, holding the pencil or chalk in a vertical position. If the material will not allow a continuous smooth line, draw broken lines close together. Ensure there is adequate space on the working surface for the marking and cutting out. Inaccuracy will result if attempting to cut out on a surface which is cluttered.

CUTTING OUT

Scissors must be sharp. It assists in controlling the scissors if the lower blade rests on a firm surface or a finger, to control it on the hand holding the material. With all material types, the cut edge should be smooth, without any notches. When cutting materials which are to be made up on the right side, for example, leather or felts which may be stab stitched, avoid at all times allowing the marking to show; cut so that these lines are cut away.

COTTONS, DRESS MATERIALS, LINENS ETC.

All these materials must be well pressed prior to cutting out.

The fabric is folded with the right side innermost and the pattern pieces are laid on the wrong side, with any marked arrows lined up with the selvedge. Be economical in the placing of your pattern pieces. If using a large patterned material the design of which may be used to complement the toy, take into consideration the design in relation to the pattern piece. For example with an animal with four legs, an elephant perhaps, the overall impact of the toy is much improved if the same part of the pattern design is selected for each leg; this does use more material but can look more effective.

FELT

This is simple to cut out as there is no right or wrong way, or side, although it is always more satisfactory to have the stretch of the fabric going across the toy.

HESSIAN

Always cut on the bias.

FUR FABRIC

Always carefully note your pile line; the arrows on pattern pieces indicate the smooth line of the pile. Fur fabric toys must have their pile laying as it would on a real animal. Be careful when you are laying your pattern pieces on to your fur fabric backing that you do not become so engrossed in placing them as economically as possible that you forget to note the arrows on the pattern pieces. It is very easy to end up with the pile in the wrong direction.

Having found your pile line, turn the fabric over with the pile side to the table and mark at one side of the backing, in tailor's chalk or pencil, an arrow marking the pile line. This will assist you in lining up your arrows on the pattern pieces. Also bear in mind that the second halves of a leg, body, head or arm all require to have their patterns reversed. Patterns can be drawn round in tailor's chalk if the fabric is a dark colour, or a soft lead pencil on a light-coloured fabric. Never use a ballpoint pen if the

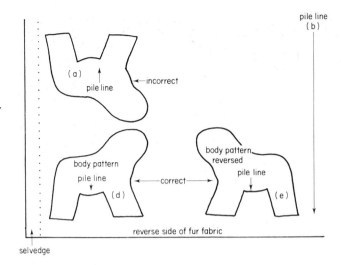

DIAGRAM 5 Laying pattern pieces onto fur fabric. **(a)** Incorrect. Pile line is in wrong direction. Always match up the pile line on the pattern pieces with the pile line of the material. **(b)** Always mark with a pencilled or chalked arrow the pile line on the backing of the fur fabric as a reminder of the pile direction. **(c)** Most fur fabric materials have a soft selvedge edge; when placing pattern pieces avoid this weak edge. **(d)** and **(e)** Correct

toy is to be washable or is light in colour as the ink will show through on its surface.

Mark any annotations on to your material pattern pieces; then you are ready for the next stage.

CUTTING FUR FABRIC

Never cut the fur fabric as you would an ordinary, thin dress-type material. You must allow for the pile, which can be so easily cut and spoiled. The way to avoid this is to lift the backing slightly with the pile still lying face down on the table, then cut by only snipping the foundation material, not the pile. As you cut, slide the point of your scissors through the material backing, thus parting any pile with which the scissors may come into contact. Turn your fabric (when a curve in pattern demands) to your scissors. Do not turn your scissors at angles as this can result in the pile being damaged.

PINNING AND STITCHING

Felt
Usually stitched on right side with a small running stitch, or stab stitched.

Cottons and printed fabrics
Can be machine stitched then turned to the right side; always snip into the fabric at the corners before turning.

Hessian
It is usually advisable to stitch along the seam line and back again to form a double row.

Velvets
Either machine stitched or back stitched.

Courtelle fleece
Machine stitched.

Fur fabrics
It is preferable for all fur fabric toys to be hand stitched; it takes a while longer but the result is far superior to a machine stitched toy. Back stitch about 0.7cm (¼in) from the cutting line. Provided you have a good, strong pile on your fabric it should be possible to have a finished toy with invisible seams. The method of achieving this is as follows. Lay the cut out

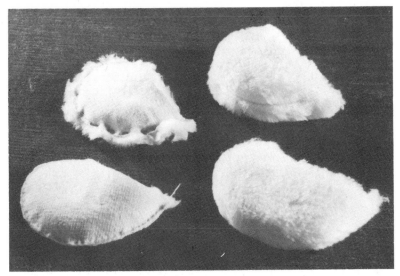

1. *Top left:* the ear is pinned incorrectly with the pile caught between the edges. *Top right:* the result of bad pinning; the fur pile is caught inside and shows a definite seam. *Bottom left:* a well stitched ear, no fur pile caught between the edges. *Bottom right:* a well-shaped ear, no seaming showing

pieces of the toy together with right sides facing. With the first finger of your left hand, as you pin the pieces of the toy together, push the fur pile in with your finger so that only the edge of the fabric shows, with no pile caught between the edges on the wrong side. When using pins count how many you insert into the toy so that you check and remove the same number. Coloured headed pins are useful in fur fabric. Back stitch and remove the pins as you stitch.

When stitching a toy with a gusset always stitch from nose to tail, then go back to the nose and stitch the other side. If you stitch all round a toy with a gusset it is easy to pull toys out of shape. Continue back stitching until you only have the stuffing opening left, then turn the toy to the right side and stuff firmly. When turning a toy to the right side, do pay special attention to the extremities of the toy, i.e. noses, hands, etc. It is so annoying to stuff a toy and then find the toy was not turned inside out correctly, with perhaps a pointed nose tucked in; it then has to be unstuffed and started again.

Just prior to stuffing it may be necessary to cut and ease the materials in any sharp corners or curves. When the toy is turned to the right side you will notice that at the corners and curves it pulls the toy out of its original shape, so snip into the curves, but only with small cuts; if you cut too deeply it will weaken the seams. On the outside curves cut two snips at angles and cut out small triangles. The reason for this is the pull on the outer curve is stronger than on the inner curve. The opening is closed with ladder stitching, which is the most useful of all stitches used in toymaking.

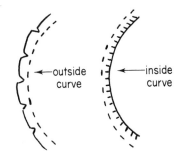

DIAGRAM 6 Cutting areas for outside and inside curves

Cotton stockinette

This jersey-type material is ideal for a doll's body as it is flexible, although great care should be taken at the stuffing stage to create the shaping. This material can be hand- or machine-stitched, or a combination of both. For example, the outside toy shape can be machine stitched and, after it is stuffed, the dimples at knees, elbows, etc. hand stitched. (See needlemodelling, Ch. 8.)

TOYS MADE FROM PATCHWORK

Toys with great character and attractive colouring can be made from scraps of fabric. They may be as simple or complicated in construction as the toymaker chooses, and easily hand- or machine-sewn. Select where possible fabrics which do not fray or stretch, such as cotton types; the material should have a firm weave.

If the toy is to be completely washable then do not mix washed and un-washed fabrics as shrinkage may occur; it is advisable to wash it all first if in any doubt. Always use a fine needle and thread and sharp scissors.

The first attempt at patchwork toymaking can just be by using squares of fabric, either matching the colour tones of the materials or a random kaleidoscope of colour. Once confidence has been gained there are many excellent books on the traditional named patchworks, with patterns that can be selected to add charm and character to the toy. A useful way of selecting the colouring or patchwork type is to obtain a piece of polystyrene foam as large as your finished article is to be and pin the cut-out patchwork pieces onto the foam, which can then be rearranged as required until the desired effect is achieved.

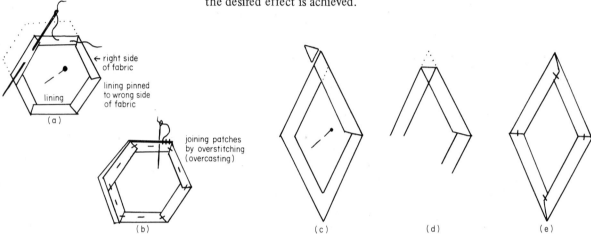

Machine-worked patchwork

To cut out the patchwork pieces — for example starting with the basic square — mark your squares on the wrong side of the fabric following the straight grain. (This can be done with a ruler and pencil.) Then cut them out allowing 0.95cm ($\frac{3}{8}$in) for seam allowances on all sides. Cut other patches from this first pattern. A cardboard template can be made, or for the more complicated shapes there are excellent metal templates available. (See back for stockists.) More than one patch at a time can be cut out by placing the template on several thicknesses of fabric.

Then machine stitch the patches together, with the right sides facing, into a strip or into pieces of material to the size required for your toy design. When finished, press open the seams with an iron and tie off and cut the ends of the thread.

Hand-sewn patchwork

Use a fine needle and thread to blend with the patches. Hand-sewn patches are formed round paper shapes cut from the template of whatever patchwork design is being used. If a firm backing is required, interfacing can be used instead of paper. The weight of paper suitable is comparable to a greaseproof or tracing paper; if too flimsy it will tear. The paper lining patches are approximately 0.7cm (¼in) smaller than the fabric patch.

Cut out two or three paper patches at a time, not more, as the paper may move and the result would be inaccurate shapes. Next, cut out the fabric patches as described for machine-worked patchwork, then pin a paper lining to the wrong side of the patchwork placed in the centre. Fold over the turnings all round and tack (baste) down, neatly folding the corners. On the corners make sure the material fits the paper lining perfectly — it will require an extra stitch at each corner to hold it — then fold down; this can be done as the patch is worked round.

The patches are then joined by overstitching (over-casting). Placing two patches right sides facing, overstitch along one whole edge at a time. Avoid stitching the paper inside and continue to join patches in this way. If a large toy is being made the patches can be joined together in units, then joined together as a whole. Press well on the wrong side and remove the tacking (basting) stitches; after this remove the papers.

Design

It is advisable when designing toys in patchwork to leave faces, feet and hands in plain coloured fabrics and the body, arms and legs of a patchwork construction. It is easier to add features onto plain fabrics. If the whole toy is made in patchwork, a face can be added by a plain felt shape stitched onto the front of the head and then features added.

Careful choice of the patchwork fabric colouring can result in most attractive designs, for example, all blue tones to simulate denim jeans on a soft doll subject. Once a range of patchwork designs are mastered and a selection of template shapes available, it can then be great fun selecting the patchwork shape to complement the toy design. For example, the clamshell patchwork can look most attractive in brown tones of fabrics to make a tortoise. Suffolk puff patchwork can also look delightful as a shell on a tortoise.

Patchwork balls

Balls can be made in felt from five-sided shapes — pentagons. They are stitched on the wrong side, then turned and stuffed. Six pentagons form one half of a ball. Make two duplicate halves, then stitch them together, leaving an opening to turn and stuff. If using appliqué motifs the article can be greatly enhanced if the colours complement one another; this requires careful colour planning before cutting out the material shapes. Easter balls using shades of yellow, orange and green are attractive. A combination of fabrics, for example a felt ball with appliquéd fur fabric animals, can look most effective.

Fur fabric pentagons are excellent for making 'roundy' toys for babies. This is also a useful way of using up fur fabric oddments which often remain after making fur fabric toys.

Strung circle toys

Strung circle toys are based on Suffolk puff patchwork. The only deviation is that the circles of the toys are gathered without a hem then strung on elastic, whereas Suffolk puff patchwork circles are hemmed, then

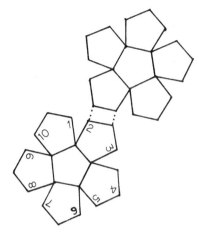

DIAGRAM 8 Pentagon ball construction. Join sides **1** and **2**, **3** and **4**; continue this until all the sections have been joined. Treat the second half of the ball likewise. Join both halves of the ball together leaving an opening to stuff, then close the opening. A tinkler can be added at the stuffing stage, or if the ball is to be a pram hanging toy add ribbons and a bow for ornamentation and to secure it

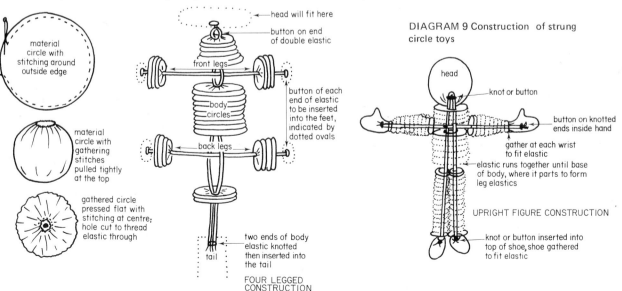

material circle with stitching around outside edge

material circle with gathering stitches pulled tightly at the top

gathered circle pressed flat with stitching at centre; hole cut to thread elastic through

head will fit here

button on end of double elastic

front legs

body circles

button of each end of elastic to be inserted into the feet, indicated by dotted ovals

back legs

two ends of body elastic knotted then inserted into the tail

tail

FOUR LEGGED CONSTRUCTION

DIAGRAM 9 Construction of strung circle toys

head

knot or button

button on knotted ends inside hand

gather at each wrist to fit elastic

elastic runs together until base of body, where it parts to form leg elastics

UPRIGHT FIGURE CONSTRUCTION

knot or button inserted into top of shoe, shoe gathered to fit elastic

23

joined side by side in patchwork form. Circle toys are an excellent medium for using up material oddments but try and keep to matching fabric weight and avoid thin material circles squashed between heavy ones, which spoils the overall balance and appearance of the toy.

STITCHES

Ladder stitching
This is not only used for closing an opening but also for attaching ears, tails, limbs, etc. It is simply a running stitch taken first on one side of an opening and then on the other, leaving the same seam allowance as you left on the rest of the toy, usually 0.7cm (¼in). The raw edges then turn themselves in neatly inside and, because of the pile you pushed inside when originally stitching, the seams become invisible. Felt will not turn in as naturally as fur fabric when ladder stitching, so it is essential to encourage it to fold in for the first few stitches, then it will turn without any problems. With any stitching in toymaking do try always to use a sewing thread to match the material being worked.

LADDER STITCH

broken lines indicate
the direction of stitches
under the sewing surface

Back stitch
Bring the needle out a stitch length in front of each stitch, then go back one stitch length. The needle should always go back into the hole made by the previous stitch.

BACKSTITCH

enlargement of back stitch

RUNNING STITCH

Running stitch
Pick up a few stitches on your needle, pull the needle and thread through the material and repeat.

French knot
Bring the thread out at A where you require the finished knot to be. Holding the thread firmly with the left hand wrap the thread firmly over the needle several times depending on the finished size of required knot. Take the needle point back into a spot near to A; pull through and fasten off.

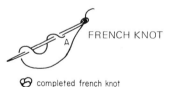

FRENCH KNOT

completed french knot

Stab stitch
Take the needle through the front of the material piece to the back piece making small stitches. This gives a broken line of stitching similar to the spacing of running stitch.

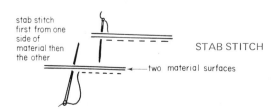

stab stitch
first from one
side of
material then
the other

STAB STITCH

two material surfaces

Double cross stitch

(a) Stitch a cross placing one stitch at right angles to the other. Out at 1, in at 2, out at 3, in at 4.
(b) Place a diagonal stitch 5—6.
(c) Place another diagonal stitch 7—8.

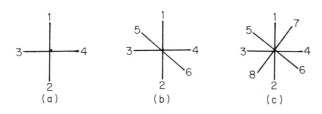

DIAGRAM 11 Double cross stitch

STUFFING TOYS

After cutting out and sewing the toy comes the stuffing stage, which is a most important feature of toymaking. However well an article is cut out and sewn, bad stuffing methods can spoil the finished toy and shorten its life considerably. So often people cut out the material, sew it well, and then take large handfuls of toy filling and push it into the article any-old-how, sometimes stretching it in all directions. Consequently the finished toy will look hard and mis-shapen with very little character. It is much better to take small quantities of filling and let the article 'breathe'. If the filling is very lumpy and compacted, fluff it out before inserting it, but the toy should not be understuffed as the stuffing will shrink to a certain extent with wear.

Method

After completing the stitching clip any seams and turn the toy skin to the right side. When stuffing a toy it should be moulded to the toy skin from within. Use your left hand to hold the part being stuffed and stuff with the right hand. The left hand can be used as a firm backing to push and mould against. A thick piece of dowelling or a wooden knitting needle is ideal for using as a stuffing stick to reach any awkward places. It helps to put a V notch in the end of the stuffing stick. Start filling the awkward places first, for example a nose point, with small quantities of filling, then broaden out to the head or body bulk. Continue working from any extremities to the main body bulk. The filling must be firm, and when the stuffing is finished up to the skin stuffing opening, partly ladder stitch the opening and insert more filling. Continue to close the opening and insert more filling until the toy outline is completed; add a final amount of filling and close the opening. If you are making a large toy it is advisable to leave it

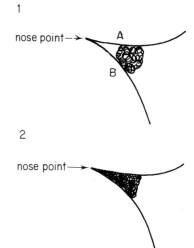

DIAGRAM 12 Stuffing a pointed nose.
1. If stuffing with large amounts of filling it forms a complete blockage at A—B, thus the nose point is empty.
2. Small amounts of filling can reach right into the nose point. Increase the size of the amounts of filling slightly as the toy bulk opens out

METHOD (A) HEAD SEPARATE FROM BODY, LADDER STITCHED TO BODY AFTER STUFFING
numbering indicates the order of placing of toy filling

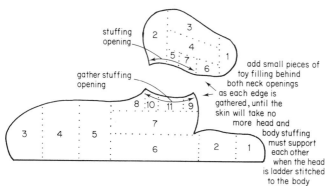

DIAGRAM 13 Adjusting stuffing routine to meet the toy requirements

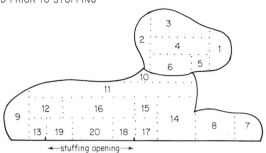

METHOD (B) HEAD DESIGNED AS PART OF THE BODY SKIN,
ATTACHED PRIOR TO STUFFING

←—stuffing opening—→

as stuffing opening is gradually closed using ladder stitching,
add small pieces of toy filling until toy skin firmly filled

overnight before sewing up the stuffing opening. This enables the filling
to settle and more filling is then added. It can sometimes be necessary to
add filling over a period of several days if the toy is very large.

Protecting stuffing openings
Temporary protection to the edges of stuffing openings can be done in
several ways.
Fur fabric: The stuffing opening can have the edges turned back and
stitched to hold.
Felt and other materials: An oval of material with a slit cut shorter than
the length of the opening on the toy can be placed over the opening and
stitched to hold. When stuffing a large toy which requires constant entering into the toy skin stuffing opening it protects the edge of the opening
to bind it by tacking a soft piece of silky material all around it. After the
filling is completed remove the binding and ladder stitch the opening
together.

DIAGRAM 14 Protecting stuffing
openings. **(a)** Tack back small turnings
either side of the opening. **(b)** Lay a
piece of material over the opening;
stitch to hold. Curve at corners — this
helps to prevent the corners of the
material curling. **(c)** Binding stitched
over the edges of the opening. A smooth,
non-clinging type of material is preferable

(a)

(b)

(c)

Closing openings
Avoid at all times overstitching an opening to close it.
Fur fabric: Ladder stitch.
Felt: If the toy has stab stitched seams, continue the stab stitching across
the opening to match the rest of the seaming.
    Many openings on soft toys are placed on an underbody. These can be
difficult to cope with. A curved needle may be the answer to this problem.

Types of filling
Kapok This is a natural material which envelopes the seeds of a tropical
tree. Use kapok behind the front skin of a rag doll's face to give a smooth
finish. It is very useful in small quantities for the points of limbs where a
firmer filling will not reach. It cannot be washed and is rather difficult to
use as its particles fly around in the atmosphere and adhere to clothes,
etc. It can help to contain the material if you hold the toy being stuffed
within a bag containing the kapok.

Synthetic filling Terylene, Dacron, Acrylics. Use these for nearly all toy-making. They are washable, lightweight and very firm. When making a large jointed toy terylene or nylon filling provides a firm body for the joints without adding weight to the body. When ordering toy filling mention that you require the loose 'opened' form to fill toys, not the impacted type used for quilting.

Foam chips Do not use these unless you wish to make a toy that will often be in water. The chips are messy and not easy to handle as they cling to any surface. They also give a toy a very lumpy appearance. Foam chips have a use if making very large cushion-type toys, where they can be used as a centre bulk filling and then encased in finer fillings. It is essential to work with the toy skin and your hands in a deep bag to avoid the filling getting everywhere; alternatively you can make a funnel from a plastic bag to prevent the chips from flying everywhere and spoiling the fabric.

Beans, lentils, polybeads Use whatever is in the larder, for example rice, tapioca, etc., for those toys requiring this type of filling, such as bean bag toys. Large cushions and toys often require more bulk. Foam granules and polybeads are lightweight and bulky, and are also ideal for floppy toys.

Sawdust and sand To ensure that a toy stands correctly the centre of gravity has to be in the feet. Sand is an excellent medium to use for a model doll's gravity. Mix some sand with wallpaper-type glue; do not make it too moist, just sufficient moisture to hold the granules together. Fill the feet whilst the leg is in an upright standing position. The sand should come to the ankle level. The feet and legs must remain in an upright position until the contents of the feet are dry. Then stuff the remainder of the legs with toy filling in the normal way. Sawdust can also be used; it is particularly suitable for a smaller doll which will not require such a heavy base.

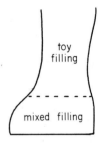

DIAGRAM 15 Centre of gravity in the feet

Foam rubber This is useful in sheet form for bathtub toys. It can be purchased in various thickness in several colours. The toy can be constructed by cutting strips out of the foam rubber for arms, legs, body and head which are then trimmed to the required shape. The shaped pieces are strung together using thread and a strong needle. The hair is fashioned from cut pieces of foam glued to the head. Features can be produced by basic needle-modelling. The second method for using foam rubber is to make the doll and cover it with a washable material. The foam rubber doll then becomes the filling.

WIRING TOYS
You cannot expect stuffing to do all the work of supporting a toy, and with a long limbed creature the stuffing requires help. Toys can be supported by wiring them with copper or galvanised wire about the size of a number 12 or 13 (USA 1 or 0) knitting needle. Choose the weight of the wire supports according to the toys' requirements. Fuse wire, pipe cleaners and millinery wires all have their uses. When wiring a toy first take the pattern and decide where most strength is needed. A horse, for example, requires supporting at neck, legs and also body. If you imagine that the wires are the skeleton of the toy it should give you an indication of where the wires should be placed, according to the work they are required to do.

Method
Measure the length of wire required to fit the toy where it needs support. Double this length. Any cut ends should be away from the top or bottom of the toy. Always bend the ends back on themselves. In a standing toy measure from half-way up the body down the back leg, up across the middle of the body, down the front leg and back up to just above the

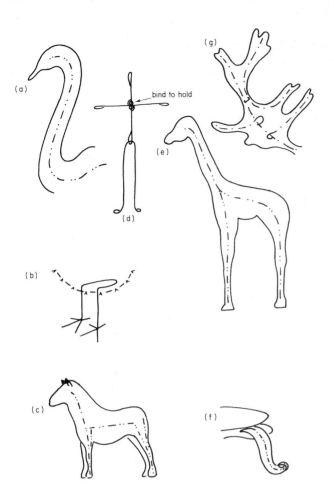

bind to hold

(a)

(g)

(e)

(d)

(b)

(c)

(f)

DIAGRAM 16 *Left* Wiring, showing areas requiring support. **(a)** Swan's neck; **(b)** chick's feet; **(c)** horse frame; **(d)** wire armature frame for making a figure; **(e)** giraffe frame; **(f)** snake's tongue; **(g)** antlers

DIAGRAM 17 *Below* Supporting a hand with pipe cleaners. **(a)** felt hand; **(b)** pipe cleaners inserted between hand pieces; **(c)** hand stab stitched on right side to hold pipe cleaners in place. Pipe cleaners can also be inserted at their full length into combined arms and hands, or legs and feet

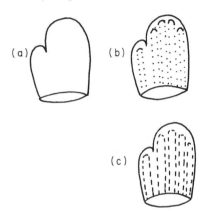

(a)

(b)

(c)

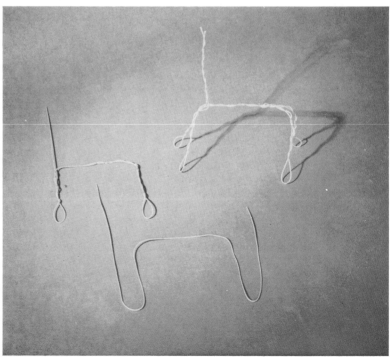

2. The front wire shape is laid out to the toy size. *Top left:* twisted to form half the framework. *Top right:* the two halves joined to form a frame

28

3. The front covered curved wire is for inserting into a toy which requires leg supports only. *Top left:* frame covered with electrical tape. *Top right:* frame covered with stuffing and bound with thread. Back legs show how to start covering the whole frame with strips of sheeting

middle of the body. Cut this length in wire; this is half the frame. Cut a duplicate piece and twist the legs as in fig. 2. Treat the other measured wire in the same manner. Join the two half pieces together by twisting to join at the neck. Loop the end pieces together to secure both together. The framework should now be taped for safety, paying particular attention to the ends. Alternatively, the two half pieces can be taped separately, then bound together. It is advisable then to cover the taped wires with sheeting cut into strips bound round the taping and stitched into place. If you wish to add thickness prior to binding with the sheeting, wrap round strips of foam or toy filling, then bind tightly with thread. Finally stitch strips of tape or sheeting over this.

The feet of the toy are then stuffed and the framework inserted. Carefully stuff round the framework with small quantities of toy filling, being sure you do not alter the shape of the toy skin. Gradually build up the filling until the toy is satisfactorily stuffed. If your toy animal only requires localised support, say, in the legs, the wire is measured from one leg base across the toy and down into the opposite leg base. Then bend the wire into an oval. The arch formed acts as a spring which when bound and prepared adds strength to the legs.

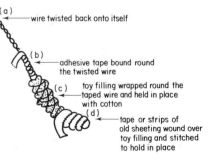

(a) — wire twisted back onto itself

(b) — adhesive tape bound round the twisted wire

(c) toy filling wrapped round the taped wire and held in place with cotton

(d) tape or strips of old sheeting wound over toy filling and stitched to hold in place

DIAGRAM 18 Preparation of a covered wire

Rag dolls

The necks of rag dolls may be thin in design and require extra support. Dowelling can be used, and this must be as well prepared as the wiring. A kitchen towel cardboard inner roll can be cut down the middle lengthways, then cut to the depth required for the support. Insert toy filling inside the cut tube, then bind the whole tube firmly. This makes an ideal support, provided the toy is not to be washable, otherwise an empty plastic washing-up liquid bottle can be cut and used. Not all rag dolls need neck supports, as some are designed to be floppy. When designing a rag doll remember that sometimes all that is necessary to provide neck support is to add two gussets, one on each side of the head, or a continuous gusset. (See design section.)

If making small dolls which require bendable limbs, perhaps to doll's house size, the most valuable method is to use pipe cleaners. They come complete with their own covering, which aids the stuffing of small limbs.

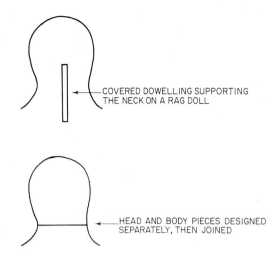

COVERED DOWELLING SUPPORTING
THE NECK ON A RAG DOLL

HEAD AND BODY PIECES DESIGNED
SEPARATELY, THEN JOINED

arrows indicate line of paper to produce
a continuous gusset for the head and shoulders

folded tracing paper

(a)(b)(c)
(b)(c)

head
(c)
(b)

shoulder

(a)

DESIGNING A HEAD GUSSET TO AVOID
NECK WRINKLING ON A RAG DOLL

DIAGRAM 19 (a) Neck supports on a
rag doll

Pipe cleaners are also excellent for inserting into the fingers of toys and puppets to make them bendable.

MAKING BASES
When making toys there are many occasions when bases are used, whether it is at the bottom of a body, the base of shoes or the base of a toy. The majority of pattern instructions recommend that the toymaker cuts a cardboard piece to line the base 0.7cm (¼in) smaller than the base pattern, but when the base is sewn into the pattern piece being lined a problem develops: the cardboard base moves or does not fit very well, and this spoils the finished article. One way to prevent this fault is to cut the cardboard to the size of base required. Cover this with the material in which the toy is being made. Glue this material cover round the cardboard base with the excess material rough edge inside the toy. Insert this prepared base, turning the rough edge of the body neatly inside. Oversew the edge of the cardboard covered base to the edge of the body. With a felt base or a felt toy a variation is used. Glue the cardboard to the felt shape of the base and do not turn in the outside edge but stab stitch it into the toy.

It adds charm and authenticity to an animal toy if, after adding the base to feet, you add such markings as claws, pads, etc. (See the section on feet for further information.)

WEIGHTED BASE TUMBLING TOYS
Weighted balls which return to their original upright position after being pushed over are great fun. They must be carefully balanced, and great care taken over the safety factors; the tumbling toy requires a large stone, a piece of lead or a piece of plasticine (modelling clay) to act as a weight, approximately the size of a golf ball, so it is essential that the weighting material is well covered and safely inserted into the toy.

Method
Gather a circle of strong cotton-type material and insert the weight. Gather the top of the material lightly, then secure this covered weight into the ball at the base. This is easier if you have the ball inside out when stitching the covered weight into place. Most ball-shaped tumbling toys are constructed in sections and the weight should be stitched at the base where all the sections meet at a point. It is essential that the ball sections are sewn securely at the seams; if the seams split open this would expose the covered weight. The ball is then firmly stuffed and the opening is closed. If you are making a toy with a head, make the smaller head from scaled down sections as in the larger ball. Stuff the head firmly and ladder stitch it to the top of the larger ball, making sure the larger ball body and the smaller ball head are well balanced.

It is advisable to use this type of toy under supervision, although theoretically this toy is safe as the weight is too large to be swallowed, even if the toy splits. The weight is also enclosed in a bag, which ensures additional safety, and the toy filling holds it all in place. However, it is advisable from time to time to check the stitching.

Design

A sectional ball can comprise four, six or eight sections. To calculate the finished size, the circumference is approximately three times the diameter. For example, a ball measuring 15.3cm (6in) in diameter will have a circumference of 45.9cm (18in) and each section will be 5.7cm (2¼in) across the centre of the segment. To calculate the size of the sections:

(a) Decide on the finished circumference.
(b) Draw a line AB the length of half the circumference.
(c) Draw a line across CDE at right angles to this, one-eighth of the circumference in length at the centre point.
(d) Draw an arc to join A, C and B and another A, E and B. This is the size of your segment. Eight segments will make the ball.

The balls for tumbling toys can either be gaily coloured random designs, or sections can be constructed to represent clothes on a character ball. Features are added to the smaller ball head. Accessories like hats and scarves can be added; however, it is advisable to avoid cluttering the toy with added items which could spoil the balance of the toy. It is preferable to integrate accessories and features into the basic ball design.

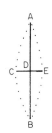

DIAGRAM 19 (b) Measuring sections of a ball

Materials

Felt is an obvious choice to use as it is colourful and does not fray. Fur fabric is ideal for tumbling animal toys. The basic balls can be constructed in sections or in patchwork designs. These toys are an excellent way of using up fur fabric oddments, cut in patchwork design then joined together. Likewise, cotton patchwork pieces can be used.

A nodding head

A nodding head adds interest to a weighted toy. You require a compressed spring available from D.I.Y. shops or ironmongers. The process of constructing the body ball is as already described. The body ball sections are left open at the top of the ball where the sections meet in a point. The body ball is firmly stuffed. The spring is covered with felt to match the character of the toy; for example, pink felt if the spring is to be a neck. Insert the covered spring well down into the body ball through the open pointed top. Ladder stitch firmly to close the ball opening and to hold the covered spring in place. The top of the covered spring is inserted into the head ball, leaving 2.5cm (1in)—5cm (2in) as the wobbling neck, between head and body. Ladder stitch the head firmly to the covering on the spring as you did at the body top.

Plastic ball base tumbling toy

Another method for making a tumbling toy is to cut a hollow plastic play ball in half using the moulded seam line as a guide to a cutting line. If you have children who play in a garden with their plastic balls and you have rose bushes you will not need to purchase a ball for this toy because you should have plenty of punctured balls available!

Method Take a lump of plasticine sufficiently heavy to hold the half ball upright and balanced. Cover with a cloth bag as previously described and glue to the inside of the base. Add some sticky-backed adhesive tape to assist it to stay in place. There are now two ways of constructing your ball toy:

(a) Cut a circle of felt large enough to cover the ball half. Gather round the top of the felt circle and lay the weighted ball half in the centre of the circle. Pull up the gathers, fasten off, and turn the gathering into the

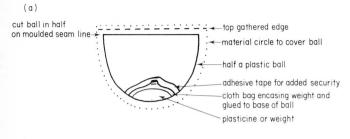

(a)

cut ball in half
on moulded seam line →

- top gathered edge
- material circle to cover ball
- half a plastic ball
- adhesive tape for added security
- cloth bag encasing weight and glued to base of ball
- plasticine or weight

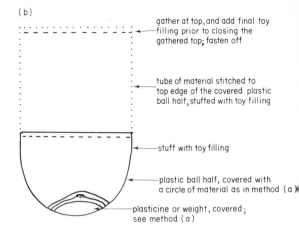

(b)

- gather at top, and add final toy filling prior to closing the gathered top; fasten off

- tube of material stitched to top edge of the covered plastic ball half, stuffed with toy filling

- stuff with toy filling

- plastic ball half, covered with a circle of material as in method (a)

- plasticine or weight, covered; see method (a)

DIAGRAM 20 **(a)** Weighted base
tumbling toys. Method **(a)**

DIAGRAM 20 **(b)** Weighted base
tumbling toys. Method **(b)**

inside of the top edge of the ball and glue into place. Press the gathers evenly as you work to give a neat appearance to the ball. Prepare the second half of the ball in the same way but omitting the weight. Stuff both balls firmly and ladder stitch both halves together round the centre. Decorate as required.

(b) Prepare the base ball with the weight and cover with material as described in (a). Instead of covering the second half of the ball you measure round the top of the weighted body base ball, and add 0.7cm (¼in) to the measurement to allow for a seam. Make a tube by sewing the short ends of the tube together on the wrong side. Turn to the right side and fasten off. Stitch one end of this stitched tube to the top of the base ball. Gather the top of the tube and, before closing, stuff firmly with a light-weight toy filling. Pull up the gathered edge and close. Decorate according to the character being made. A point to note is that whilst the circumference of your tube is determined by the size of the ball being used, the actual depth of the tube can be adjusted slightly to suit the character of the toy. Beware, however, of extending the tube too much or the toy will become top heavy.

Weighting a toy to balance

Sometimes, however well a toy is stuffed — perhaps because of faulty designing — it can be top heavy, especially a sitting toy. This can be rectified by weighting inside the toy at the bottom of the back; plasticine (modelling clay) is suitable for this or a solid piece of wood, provided it is well covered.

ADDING MUSICAL UNITS

The musical box

The musical clockwork mechanism was first invented in 1796 by a Genevese name Antoine Favre. Geneva then became the main centre for the development and production of fine musical boxes. By 1811 production had moved to the swiss town of Sainte-Croix high in the Jura mountains. The Reuge factory, which began producing fine musical boxes in the nineteenth century, is the largest musical box manufacturer in Switzerland, making a range of movements from the small 18-note ones to the largest made in the world, the 144-note movement.

Musical units

Toys with musical units are certainly expensive to buy, but they do make delightful special gifts. Most units are either the key-wind or the pull-cord method. These are inserted into the toy when it is almost completely stuffed. The key or pull wind protrudes from the back of the toy through the stuffing opening; you then add the final stuffing making sure you do not interfere with the key or cord movement. Then ladder stitch the opening as usual. It adds support to the unit if it is enclosed in a net bag and sewn to the skin of the toy, as described next for growlers and squeakers.

Growlers and squeakers

These are inserted at the front or back centre of the teddy or toy. On growlers you will find the front has small holes like the top of a pepper pot; these must be facing the wall of the toy and sewn to it. Stuff round it very firmly to hold it in place. Growlers are either metal or plastic cylinders; the growler is ideal for the larger teddy, a squeaker is sufficient for a small toy. The squeak is produced by a reed in a small cylinder, and the reed end must be placed against the skin of the toy. With continual wear and movement the growler or squeaker can easily move, so it must be secured into position. Place it in a bag made of terylene or a similar net material. (Also suitable are the small mesh net bags used in supermarkets as containers for carrots, nuts, etc.) The material should be such as to enable the sound to come through clearly.

Tinklers

A tinkler is mainly used in roly-poly toys as it consists of steel pins of different lengths, with weights at one end, when the tinkler is rotated the weights hit the pins and produce the sound. Most tinklers these days are made of plastic and are completely waterproof. If inserted into ordinary toys it is not necessary to secure them except with firm stuffing.

DIAGRAM 21 *Below, left* Choosing the correct joint size for a toy, and where to place a growler in a bear. **(a)** The neck disc should fit without altering the shape of the head line. **(b)** Always choose a joint size which is as large as the toy skin will allow. Leave sufficient space surrounding the covered joint to allow for stuffing and stitching up the limb opening. **(c)** The net bag encasing the growler is stitched to the back skin of the bear. Holes in the growler face outwards.

4. *Top:* a pull/wind musical box unit. *Right:* a key wind musical unit. *Left:* a growler. *Bottom:* squeaker

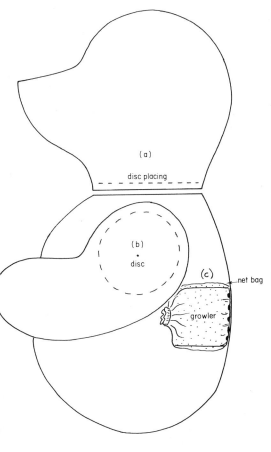

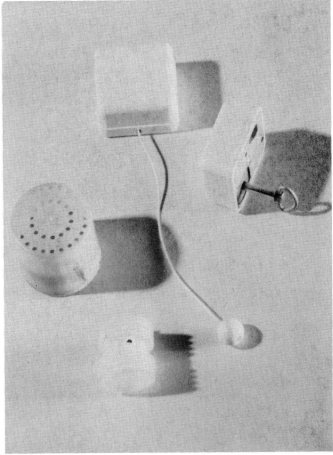

TOYS WITH JOINTS

You only have to visit a museum with a dolls' section and you can see the various methods of jointing which have developed over the years. Hinging, gussets, rivets, ball and socket — all these methods have made it possible for the limbs and bodies of dolls to move. The earlier bisque dolls had soft leather bodies with gussets, and were filled with such materials as sawdust, wood-wool, cork and bran. Many of these dolls also had hinged joints — for example, the Ne Plus Ultra joint which was patented by Sara Robinson. The Universal joint was patented in 1896. Disc jointing was patented at the turn of the century. Many of the earlier jointing methods were complex and unattractive, but as soft toys gradually replaced many of the beautiful composition dolls, the present day disc and stitching methods became more common.

Stitched hinging

To enable a rag doll to be jointed and to take the roughest treatment, the best method to articulate the toy is possibly to stitch hinge it. This can be a very simple process in its more basic form or it can be used to produce a more intricate toy.

First to discuss the general basic approach. All that is required is an unstuffed rag doll consisting of head, body, legs and arms. Stitch all the pattern pieces, turn to right sides leaving the top of legs, arms and base of head open. At this stage leave the top and bottom of the body open as the treatment of the body varies according to the hinging method used.

Starting with the arms you place a small amount of toy filling into the hands, then stab stitch to indicate the fingers. (See diagram for correct placing.) Continue to stuff arms; if you require a wrist gather underneath the hand at the wrist and fasten off. Firmly and smoothly stuff to the elbow. Stab stitch across from side to side of the arm to make the elbow. Stuff to within about 2.5cm (1in) of the top of the arm. (This measurement will vary according to the size of the doll being made.) Then stab stitch across, leaving the top free from any filling. This will be joined to the doll's body at the shoulder later.

Deal with the legs in the same manner. They are stuffed firmly to the knee then, with the centre front seam placed to the centre back seam, the leg is stab stitched across from side to side to make the knee hinge. The top of the leg will be stitched across leaving a section free from toy filling. This will be stitched to the base of the body or inserted into the base of it, depending on method being used. Whatever hinging is being applied to the toy being made, always turn the open top of the limbs in neatly before applying to the body.

Single hinge dolls

These are stitched across (hinged) at shoulders and hips. You can also make a body and headpiece all in one and can add arms and legs by inserting them in the seam openings, and machining or hand stitching across.

Double hinging

This is the single hinge stitching plus additional hinging at elbows and knees, i.e. hinged elbows and knees, and hinged shoulders and hips.

Always make sure the thumbs of the arms are placed to the front of the toy, and similarly when inserting the legs into the base of the body ensure the feet face to the front. When stitching a rag doll's legs, add small pleats at each side of the top of the leg to avoid them sticking out sideways as a result of the stitching and so spoiling the line of the leg.

Waist hinge

Should you require the maximum movement, the doll can also be stitched across at the waistline. Added flexibility can be achieved by leaving an unstuffed area at the waist level and stitching twice across to contain the stuffing at the top and bottom of the body.

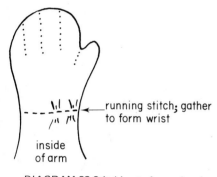

running stitch; gather to form wrist

inside of arm

DIAGRAM 22 Stitching to form a hand

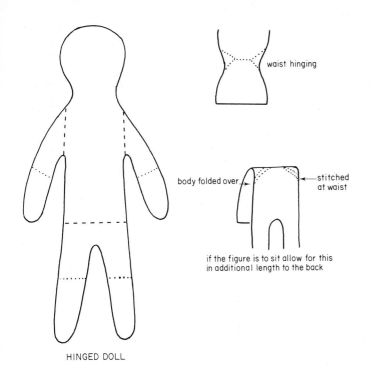

waist hinging

body folded over → ← stitched at waist

if the figure is to sit allow for this in additional length to the back

HINGED DOLL

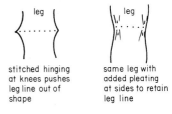

DIAGRAM 23 Stitched hinging. Single hinged dolls are stitched across (hinged) at shoulders and hips. (See broken line.) Double hinged dolls have additional hinging at elbows and knees, indicated by dotted lines

leg

stitched hinging at knees pushes leg line out of shape

leg

same leg with added pleating at sides to retain leg line

neck

arrow indicates ridge; shaded area is where thumb has pressed

side body seam

Socket shoulder hinge

After you have made and stuffed a toy body, press your thumb at the side of the body — at the top just below the shoulder — until you have pushed up a ridge at right angles to the side of the body seam. Attach the top of the arm to the ridge. (See diagram.)

Lap hinge

With this method the top of the arm is left unstuffed. The top of the arm is turned in and stitched across to the shoulder, with the arm hanging down by the side of the body. To enable a correct lap hinge it is necessary to stitch the shoulders on the body into a square shape. This can be achieved by two different methods.

Method 1 Pull the body skin just below the shoulder at the front (chest) and the back of the toy (before you turn it to the right side). You then fold down the shoulder point and stitch. Turn to right side and apply the arm with a lap hinge.

DIAGRAM 25 Hinging: socket shoulder hinge

DIAGRAM 24 Hinging: lap hinge

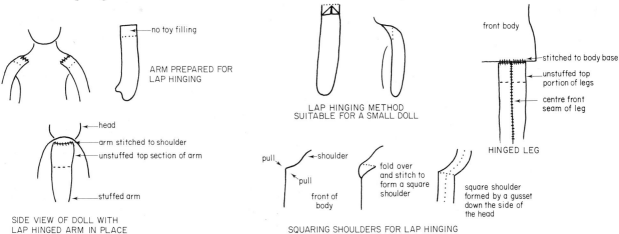

no toy filling

ARM PREPARED FOR LAP HINGING

head

arm stitched to shoulder

unstuffed top section of arm

stuffed arm

SIDE VIEW OF DOLL WITH LAP HINGED ARM IN PLACE

LAP HINGING METHOD SUITABLE FOR A SMALL DOLL

pull ← shoulder

pull

front of body

fold over and stitch to form a square shoulder

square shoulder formed by a gusset down the side of the head

SQUARING SHOULDERS FOR LAP HINGING

front body

stitched to body base

unstuffed top portion of legs

centre front seam of leg

HINGED LEG

fold in the sides
of the leg, then lay
front edge over back
edge and stitch

DIAGRAM 26 **(a)** Hinging: parcel hinge

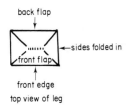

back flap

sides folded in

front flap

front edge

top view of leg

DIAGRAM 26 **(b)** Hinging: parcel hinge

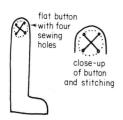

flat button
with four
sewing
holes

close-up
of button
and stitching

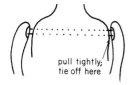

pull tightly,
tie off here

DIAGRAM 27 Hinging: pivot jointing,
method 2

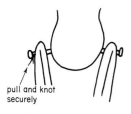

pull and knot
securely

Method 2 To achieve a square shoulder add a gusset down the side of the head and shoulder. (See diagram.) On a small toy a neat lap hinge can be formed by folding the top of the arm. (See diagram.)

Gusset joints
These are designed so that neither the elbows nor the knees can bend forward in the wrong direction. They require careful construction, especially at the stuffing stage, to ensure the stuffing does not distort the gusset joint. The joint is made by a slit being cut in the knee and elbow into which a gusset is inserted.

Parcel hinge
You only stitch the front edge of the legs to the front edge of the body; this enables the toy to bend forward. See diagram for the method of folding the top of the leg into a parcel hinge; the body base is folded in the same way.

Flange to permit rotation of the head
When modelling a head to fit a cloth body a flange (ridge) is added to the base of the neck. This is inserted into the neck of the cloth body, which is then gathered to fit the moulded neck above the flange. The body is well stuffed and the head then rotates within the gathered neck.

Pivot hinged dolls
This is an early version of jointing a toy and should be mentioned; however, current safety regulations regarding toy making standards would not permit its use. Whilst this method is very suitable for a stylized toy being made as a collector's item, it is not safe in a toy to be used by a young child. The elastic could break and this would free the shanked buttons, which could then be easily swallowed.

Method 1 Make the toy in the usual way, i.e. stitching and stuffing. (It makes the doll easier to joint if you do not stuff the body firmly at the outset.) Make a hole in the limb. Thread the length of elastic through the shank of one button until placed centrally. Thread the two ends of the elastic through the limb, through the body and out through the opposite limb. Place another shanked button onto the ends of the elastic; finish stuffing the body firmly, making sure you do not interfere with the elastic, and pull tightly, pulling the limbs firmly to the side of the body. Knot the elastic ends tightly together and trim off the excess elastic. Complete other limbs in the same way.

Method 2 Suitable for a smaller toy. Use 2cm (¾in) to 2.5cm (1in) buttons with four sewing holes and of a flat design. The buttons are sewn on the inside of the limb, i.e. the side nearest the body. Stuff the body firmly and close. Starting with the arms, sew to the body using a double thickness of button thread. Sew first through the cross made by sewing on the buttons, but do not stitch to the arm fabric. Go straight through the body pulling tightly, then through the cross on the inside of the other arm. Continue to stitch from one side of the body to the other making sure the thread is held taut at all times. Repeat the process for the leg. It helps to make the thread tougher if, after you have threaded your needle, you rub the thread with beeswax or candlewax.

DIAGRAM 28 Hinging: pivot jointing, method 1. Shanked buttons on elastic or strong thread

Shank joints

Work buttonhole stitches over shanks of thread between body and arm. Alternatively, you can work the buttonhole stitches over a shank from the top of shoulder to the top of arm. (See diagrams.)

Another shank method is to gather the top of the stuffed arm, fasten off and then stitch threads between arm and body, leaving a gap of about 1.3cm (½in). Bind round the shank threads as you would when applying a button to a garment, then fasten off.

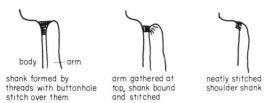

shank formed by threads with buttonhole stitch over them

arm gathered at top, shank bound and stitched

neatly stitched shoulder shank

DIAGRAM 29 Hinging: shank joints

Ne plus ultra

A joint held together by a button or washer with tight thread or cord.

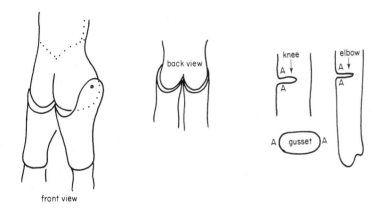

front view

back view

knee

elbow

gusset

DIAGRAM 30 Ne plus ultra joints. The original dolls in this style had French bisque swivel heads and their bodies were made of kid. They often had gusseted knees and elbows

ne plus ultra hip joint

gusset hinged knees

Combination jointing

Providing the combination of jointing methods used are suitable for the age of the recipient, it is quite acceptable to use more than one type of jointing in a toy. For example, a toy may have a disc joint for its head but may require the stitched hinge method for legs and arms. A rag doll may have firmly stuffed legs with no knee hinge, but it may be required to sit, and stitched hinging can be used to make this possible. Do not mix disc and stitched hinging on a toy which is to be washable; only use stitched hinging in that case.

Disc jointing

Each joint set comprises two hardboard or wooden discs, two metal washers and a cotter pin. Patterns tell you the size to use but if you are jointing a toy which is not jointed in the pattern, or have designed the toy yourself, the following is the way to chose the correct size.

Neck. On a large bear you need as large a joint as will comfortably fit into the neck opening. If it is too large it will form a ridge; if too small, the head will wobble after jointing. Note that joints become larger when they are covered in felt or fur fabric.

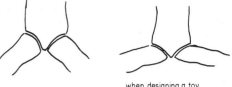

disc joint in place
laying flat between
head and body

when designing a toy
take careful note of the
angles required if disc jointing

disc joint in
place between
arm and body.
note bent cotter
pin inside body

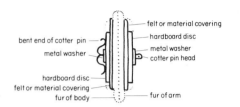

felt or material covering
hardboard disc
metal washer
cotter pin head

bent end of cotter pin
metal washer

hardboard disc
felt or material covering
fur of body

fur of arm

DIAGRAM 31 Disc jointing

cotter pin
to be inserted
into second
half of disc
inside gathered
top of body

bent cotter
pin securing
head and
body
together

DIAGRAM 32 (a) Disc jointing; method
1: The neck edge is gathered over the
disc which is inside the head; only cotter
pin ends protrude for insertion into the
top of the body disc

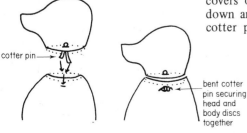

cotter pin

bent cotter
pin securing
head and
body discs
together

DIAGRAM 32 (b) Disc jointing; method
2: The disc joint is tailored to fit the
neck opening. The stitching line is the
outside edge of the previously covered
fur disc

Legs and arms. On a large bear use the same size joints for legs and arms
but larger for the neck. On a smaller bear the combination might be legs
one size, arms another, head another, especially if the toy has chubby legs.
Keep in mind the weight the joint will have to support. Avoid heavy
stuffing. Arms and leg joints must have a comfortable clearance all round
the outside edge. If they are too large they will not leave the room for
the seam of the toy to be ladder stitched together over the stuffing.

Covering joints. Dismantle the component parts of the joint. For each
joint set, cut out two circles of thick material (e.g. felt) larger all round
than discs; on a large joint 1.3cm (½in) larger, on a smaller one 0.7cm
(¼in). Gather round the outside edge of the circle with a running stitch,
pull up, make a small hole in the centre and put the disc – with the washer
and the cotter pin – inside. Gather firmly and finish off. Treat the other
half of the joint, without the cotter pin, in the same way, making a centre
hole. These gathered material circles will help pad the discs so that they
cannot be felt through the toy fabric and will also help with the wear of
the toy.

An alternative method is to cut circles of leather larger than the disc
and to place them directly against the fur fabric of the toy to mask the
sharp edges of the disc.

Jointing a head Method 1. Stuff the head firmly and gather round the neck
of the head loosely; do not secure it. Put the prepared disc with the cotter
pin facing outside. (This will later be inserted into the top of the body.)
Pull the previously partly gathered neck edge until it fits tightly round
the disc and cotter pin. Slightly open the cotter pin otherwise it is easy
to push it back into the head! Then gather the neck edge at the top of
the body. Insert the cotter pin protruding from the head through the top
of the body and through the centre of the gathered body neck edge and
thread this cotter pin through the hole in the second half of the joint;
place the second washer onto the cotter pin, always having the material
covers on the joints facing smooth sides together. Turn the toy upside
down and with pointed round nosed pliers grasp the longest end of the
cotter pin fairly low down, pulling hard upwards and then outwards,

turning it away from you into the shape shown in the diagram. Turn the toy round; pull and turn the other half of the pin away from you in like manner. These bent cotter pins act as a spring holding head and limbs in position; the joints must be held tightly together by cotter pin springs as a joint works loose in use and so it needs to start off very firm.

Jointing a head Method 2. This is more satisfactory than the previous method if the toy to be jointed is a large one. The previous method is suitable for smaller toys.

Cover the discs with fur fabric to match the fur of the toy in the same way as already described above, only gather the neck edge slightly until it is the same size as the outside edge of the fur covered disc. Fasten off, then overstitch the gathered neck edge to the edge of the joint, with the cotter pin protruding. Gather the neck edge on the body until it fits the edge of the other half of the fur covered disc, fasten off, then stitch the body neck edge to the edge of the disc. Push the cotter pin protruding from the head base through the hole in the other half of the disc and proceed as described in Method 1.

Jointing a limb. Some toy patterns have the limbs complete in shape. These can be partly stuffed and then the prepared felt covered disc can be pushed to the outside from inside the arm on the toy. (The exact position of the joint is usually marked on the pattern.) It is then inserted through the side of the body onto another prepared disc as already described for the head. Sometimes a jointed toy pattern has the top of the arm cut away. In this case cover the disc and cotter pin with the same colour fur as the arm and insert the prepared disc into position on the arm, ladder stitching it into position.

5(a). Cross section of a bear's body showing disc joints in place on the inside of the toy, with cotter pins bent to secure them

5(b). Cross section of a bear's limbs outside the body, with cotter pin heads showing

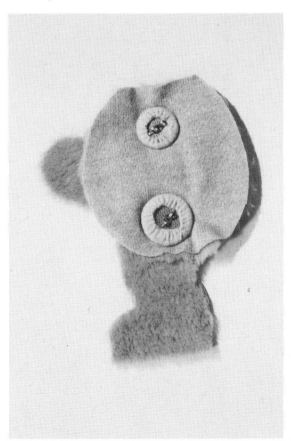

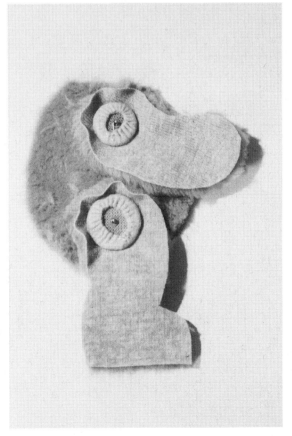

Limbs and head should always lay flat where they touch the body. Work from the top of toy, from stuffed head to stuffed arms, and lastly legs onto the unstuffed body. By working in this order there are less limbs to get in the way of your work. Last of all firmly stuff the body and sew it up. Make sure as you work that the body does not become twisted in any way. Limbs must be neatly placed on the body, not one arm shoulder height with the other at the waist! Always partly stuff a limb, then add the half joint, then finally stuff the top half of the limb and ladder stitch round the opening. If you keep straightening the body as you work it will avoid mistakes and bad placing of limbs. Some cotter pins are not very long, so always grip as low as possible before bending them into a spring. Once the knack of pull, curl and bend is achieved, further jointing will be plain sailing.

A joint should not be felt through a limb since it would eventually wear through the toy skin. If the limb on a small toy is very small, once it is jointed there may be very little space for stuffing. Always use the following method to hold the stuffing in place. When covering the discs substitute a thinner material for the limb half of the joint and make the circle of this large enough for it to encase the disc with a gathered bag into which you place the stuffing; this protects the cotter pin eye and at the same time holds the limb stuffing permanently in place. Many toy patterns are suitable for jointing providing they can be cut straight at the head, arms and legs so that the joints lay flat to the body.

Jointing need not be restricted to fur toys; rag dolls and material toys are just as satisfactory.

When designing a toy to be disc jointed the head joint will automatically be set flat on the neck of body. An arm is set and jointed parallel to the shoulder and body side, and therefore it will turn in a circle; however, the leg placing is usually at an angle due to the body shaping, therefore it will turn in that direction. Make sure your body angle and there-

6(a). Net round disc to hold the stuffing in place which will mask the disc

6(b). Stuffing in gathered net circle, disc joint hidden inside

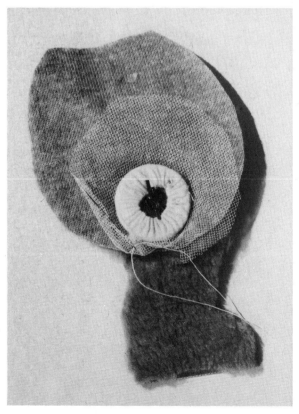
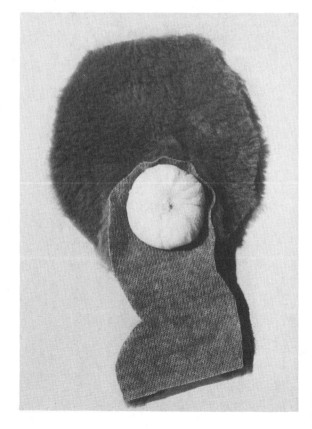

fore the disc and leg angle are suitable for the character you wish to portray, especially when designing and animal.

Some final points:

(a) Make sure the joints are the correct size.

(b) Always cover them well.

(c) Hold the joints together tightly in your left hand and always pull well on the cotter pins before twisting into a spring, first making sure the washer is pressed right down on the cotter pin and flush to the disc.

(d) When jointing a head always put more stuffing in just before the final sewing up; you will be surprised at how much stuffing can be inserted at this stage.

(e) The material cover of the disc must be smooth so that it lays flat to the other half of the disc.

(f) Always joint into the body where the bulk of the stuffing will hide the springs of the bent cotter pins.

(g) Bears and toys with shoulders are very easy to stuff inadequately across the shoulders as arm joints can act as a barrier for stuffing; the result is a very wobbly head. The joints at the neck particularly must be well supported by the stuffing. The stuffing must be packed tightly into the shoulders of the toy.

(h) There are plastic joints on the market with push-on metal washers, on the same principle as the safety lock eyes. It is an advantage that they are washable but they do not wear as well as wooden or hardboard discs.

(i) Finally, it is good policy to partly stuff a toy to be jointed, especially if it is a large one, and then leave it, as the stuffing then settles and more can be added.

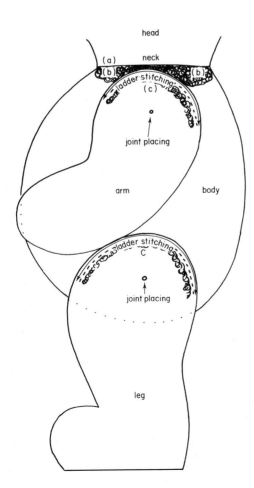

DIAGRAM 33 Parts of a toy which are often inadequately stuffed. **(a)** The neck joint will not do all the work of support; it must have very firm stuffing or the head will wobble. **(b)** The toy must be well stuffed under the neck and behind the arm joint. This stuffing has to support the neck disc and the head. Both the arm joints need the strength of the stuffing behind them. Push the stuffing well into the shoulders of the toy. **(c)** When the arms and the legs are stuffed they are then ladder-stitched to close where indicated. Here is another danger spot. Having stuffed the limbs one then stitches up the top openings, leaving insufficient stuffing under the stitching. This can be avoided by stitching half-way across the opening, then inserting small quantities of toy filling. Stitch a little further and add more filling, then before the final few stitches add tiny pieces of filling. By bilding up the filling behind the stitching it will achieve a really firm limb and, most important, a good line to the toy

5 Designing soft toys

Designing in soft toymaking is really all about shapes, and what each shape will produce in relation to the toy design. Once the shaping processes have been mastered it should be easy to achieve whatever effect is required. It is interesting to compare various toy designer's work. Whilst there are basic guideline principles, each designer adapts or alters these principles as they develop their own original methods and concepts. It is this stamp of originality which makes designing in any form so exciting. In the later sections in this book – on darts, gussets, ears, etc. – it is possible to learn various design techniques, and these can be adapted to meet your requirements. After a while you will need to rely less and less on the principles given here and develop ideas of your own. If designing is at first a problem it is possible to base your first attempts on established subjects. For example, the nest of doll Matriochkas which were for centuries made by the Russians out of carved wood have a very clear basic outline, and the photographs show how this subject was made into an embroidered toy.

To create a toy can be the most rewarding experience. Be pleased with what you create but learn to be positive in your self-criticism, and then progress should be acheved.

INSPIRATIONAL SOURCES

A toy can be based on an oval or circle shape. Most people doodle on paper, and by drawing several basic shapes you may well find that you have the start of a toy design. Add features and hair. Decide on suitably attractive material, and this basic shape could become an original and lovable toy. (The Mr Men characters are a good example of how successful basic shapes can be.) So often toymaking students greet the suggestion that they should design their own soft toys with cries of 'I cannot draw' or 'I never have any original ideas.' These problems are easily overcome. Look through illustrated children's books; these are a wonderful source of material. If the animal or doll pictures have a basic shape this can be traced and, if necessary, enlarged; you require no more than this to start.

7. Matriochkas, showing each individual item with machine embroidery

DESIGN CONSIDERATIONS

Whether designing technically or from a basic shape, certain points have to be observed and taken into consideration.

(a) Have in mind what the function of the toy is to be, whether a soft bedtime toy, a real-life toy or a model toy to be decorative in a child's bedroom. Is the toy to be dressed?

(b) Bear in mind any material you may wish to use.

(c) Is the toy to be washable or not?

(d) The safety factors in relation to the age of the recipient.

(e) Is the toy to have an elaborate construction or a basic shape?

(f) The toy's size in relation to the child.

(g) List the main features of the toy. All animals have predominating features which instantly enable the child to recognise what it is. A snail is recognised by its shell; without the shell, it resembles a slug. A donkey has large ears; with small ears it is a horse. A zebra's feature is by its stripes. Whatever the methods being used to create a soft toy it is essential to incorporate its main recognisable features. Note the size of ears in relation to the body, and the direction in which they face. Note the position of the eyes.

(h) A very important factor is whether the toy will be acceptable to the child. It is pointless to create an elaborate toy if the child requires a simple toy. Children form fantasy worlds round their toy playmates, so any play needs must be fulfilled. A toy that is too intricate can stifle the inventiveness of the child's mind.

PRINCIPLES AND METHODS OF TOY DESIGNING

All patterns should be made in paper or tracing paper, then either mounted or traced onto a card to make the pattern more durable. As each pattern piece is designed mark any annotations onto it. Do this as you build up your subject stage by stage; if you leave it to the last, you may well have forgotton some important information.

THE BASIC SHAPE

Two main principles are involved. Always start with a clear basic outline — the silhouette of the design — and proceed, when required, to develop it into three dimensions. When tracing from a book the artist may have added sharp angles which would not be suitable for the toy. Trace the outline and re-draw it but simplify the shape. Start with an animal that lies down, like a rabbit, as it is easier to cope with. Advance to functional

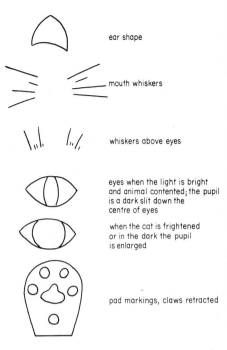

ear shape

mouth whiskers

whiskers above eyes

eyes when the light is bright and animal contented; the pupil is a dark slit down the centre of eyes

when the cat is frightened or in the dark the pupil is enlarged

pad markings, claws retracted

DIAGRAM 34 Features for a toy cat design. When designing a toy animal it is necessary to research and list the main features; this will add character and authenticity to the design

8. Nesting with the baby inside

43

legs at a later time when confidence has been gained.

Having achieved a basic shape, is it to the required size? Turn to the section on enlarging and reducing a pattern and adjust the outline size as required. Always add on 0.7cm (¼in) to allow for turnings. If using ordinary material, not fur fabric, for your first effort, lay the pattern on the material and cut it out twice. With the right sides of the material facing, pin and then machine or backstitch round the outside edge, leaving an opening — preferably at the base — to enable stuffing. Clip any tight corners, turn to right side, stuff firmly and close the opening with ladder stitching. (See relevant section for details of how to work this stitch.) The result is a flat two-piece toy. Apply the features and some trimming if required, and it could be a most suitable toy for a baby.

Using the basic outline pattern shape you started with, cut out in material again, but this time add a continuous gusset not wider than one-third of the body depth, between the body pieces from the tail along the top of the body and along the underbody back to the tail. Pin and stitch, turn to right side, stuff and close the opening; a more realistic shape has formed that is much more interesting.

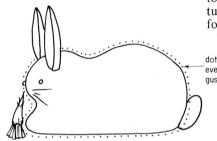

DIAGRAM 35 Examples of suitable toy designs for all round gusset

dotted line indicates even width all round gusset

gusset

add tufts of wool for the hedgehog's prickles all over the toy's back, completely covering the base material

A gusset therefore adds bulk to a toy. How to determine the width of a gusset on a more detailed toy is given later. It is only once the toy has been made up that any mistakes occur. Do try and overcome the inevitable early mistakes on the basic toy by always being careful of the choice of materials, and be imaginative in the use of braid and accessories. The toy will then at least look gay and attractive, even if it does end up with a disappointing shape. It is comforting to know that children are not going to be worried about any design faults. Try and be observant and thus avoid past errors.

It can be useful in toy design to keep each pattern piece, whether it was successful or not, the reason being, as already stated, that mistakes show up only when you see the toy stuffed and completed. List the mistakes when you reach this stage, using the finished toy as your visual aid. Draw the patterns clearly, then mark onto the patterns the areas which require alteration; the next toy made from this pattern will have had the mistakes removed. In the first flush of disappointment it is easy to discard the toy and tear up the pattern, whereas by marking the necessary alterations the next toy could be a success and the design time not the waste you originally imagined. Sometimes all that is required is an adjustment to the width or the length of the toy. Some angles on the pattern may be too acute or the positioning of the limbs incorrect. Cut your original pattern where these adjustments are required, lay these pieces onto a plain piece of paper and pin into place; this backing paper will allow you to open out and add length or width to the original pattern. When satisfied that the alterations have combated the original mistakes, re-cut the pattern piece.

ADDING LEG SHAPING TO A BASIC OUTLINE

Having mastered the basic lying toy with the added gusset, now draw a basic outline shape of a standing animal. Add a gusset, not too wide, from the base of the front leg, round over the body to the base of the back leg. A further gusset of the same width is required from the base at the back of the front legs, up around the underbody and down to the base of the inner back legs. You now have two gaps at the front and back leg bases, so it is necessary to cut another pattern piece for the leg base. To obtain the correct size for the leg base pattern measure the width of both sides of the pattern and the width of the body gusset at each end. Cut pattern pieces and stitch together as before, turn to right side and stuff. Carefully consider the toy's distinguishing features, remembering the wear the toy is to have.

Having reached this far it is good practice to obtain a notebook and list the facts you have learned. At this stage the notes may well be:

(a) Always start with a silhouette

(b) Keep the outline as uncluttered as possible and avoid sharp curves.

(c) The silhouette is flat; stuffing adds bulk but in doing so reduces the width of the toy.

(d) Add width to the basic outline which will allow for seaming and stuffing.

(e) Do not cut the toy on the bias of the material; it will become mis-shapen if you do.

(f) Carefully consider the animal's features; study the relevant sections before proceeding.

Now to discuss individual design principles. Having learned how to apply a narrow gusset of the same width round a toy, you will see by studying soft toy patterns that a gusset may start off narrow at the tail end on a toy animal, possibly to widen out under the body and chest, narrow at the neck, widen to the crown of the head and often end at the back of the neck in a point. Obviously the gusset design is determined by the shaping required. After some practice the toymaker will quickly become accustomed to looking at the picture or photograph and seeing instantly the areas which will require gussets to produce the shape. Whatever the gusset shape on a fur fabric toy, never sew a gusset from one side of the body completely round the toy and back to where you started; this would result in a twisted toy. Start out at one side of the toy — for example, on a teddy bear's head gusset — stitch from the nose to the end of the gusset, fasten off and return to the nose point on the opposite side. Start again and stitch to the end of the gusset. This will produce a well-balanced head.

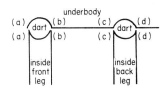

DIAGRAM 36 **(a)** Darting an underbody gusset

STANDING TOY WITH FOUR LEGS

When designing an underbody gusset for a standing toy always set the inside back and inside front legs on a dart; this will control the legs when stuffing and prevents them from splaying out. Gussets are used when it is necessary to open out a body shape and to add, for example, a fat stomach to a toy. If a rotund figure is required, start the gusset at the haunches and end above the front leg. If a wide neck is required, continue the gusset to the throat. Always obtain a good picture of the animal you are creating the toy from, and you will soon learn how to use a gusset to obtain the width required. If you want to design a head gusset on a horse first obtain a front view picture of a horse and draw or trace the silhouette. This then becomes the outline of the pattern shape. Between this shape must be a gusset to open out the pattern from a flat basic toy to one having a wide head. On the diagram of the horse's head (36(b)) one can see where the gusset has to be inserted between the head silhouettes. Taper the ends of the gusset to mould gradually into the toy skin.

Gussets can add character to the toy and must always be in proportion to the other body patterns. Underbody gussets give bulk to the finished toy. If the curve of the gusset outline is an upward-curving bulge, the toy will be fat; if cut with a downward curve the result will be a slim toy. If broadness is required in the hindquarters of a toy animal this can be achieved by extending the underbody gusset to the area where the broadness is required. To work out the correct measurements, start by measuring from A at the throat of the horse (diagram 36(d)) round the head silhouette to B at the back of the neck. The width of the head gusset at its widest place should be two-thirds the width of the head measured

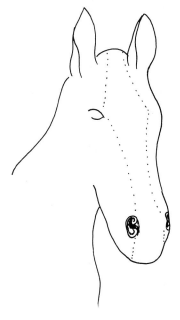

DIAGRAM 36 **(b)** Showing head gusset design

DIAGRAM 36 **(c)** The brief selection of diagrams given here is to show the reader areas which require gussets. Each animal has suitable accompanying gusset shapes. (These are not to scale). Head gussets are shown for all animals, except for the seal in the bottom right-hand corner, where an underbody gusset is marked

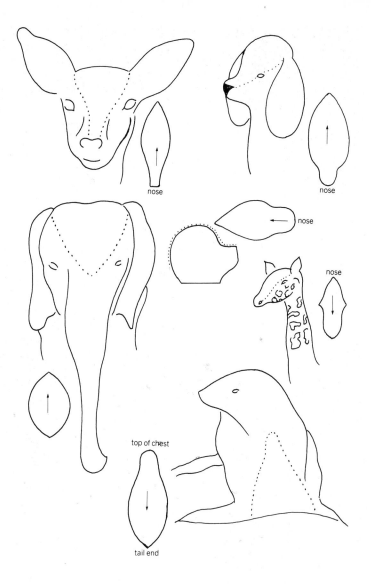

nose

nose

nose

nose

top of chest

tail end

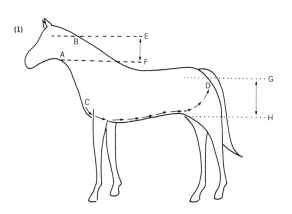

(1)

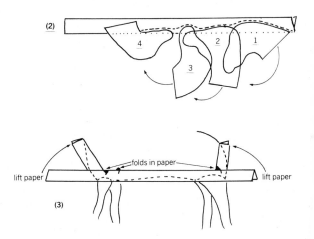

(2)

(3)

folds in paper

lift paper

lift paper

DIAGRAM 36 **(d)** Designing head and underbody gussets

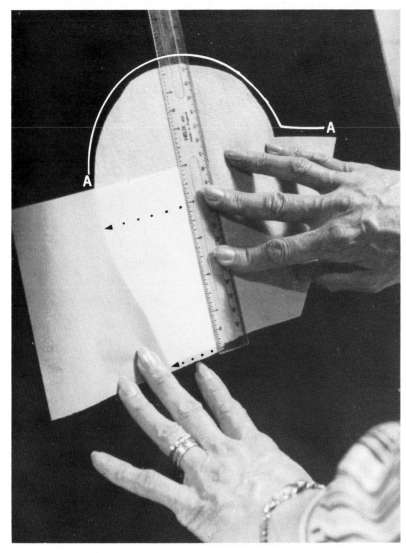

9. Measuring a head gusset on a bear. The length of the gusset is line A–A (over the top of the head). The width of the gusset in its widest place is half the width of the profile head measured from the top of the head to the base of the neck, indicated on the figure by dotted lines

E–F on diagram. Take a piece of tracing paper. The length of the paper is the measurement you obtained by measuring A–B, and the width of paper the measurement E–F. Fold the paper in half lengthways with the folded edge facing towards you. Following moves 1, 2, 3 and 4 in the diagram, swivel and move the head pattern forwards, and as you do so draw round the head outline where indicated by a broken line. When the throat area is reached (the fourth move), remove the head pattern, cut off the excess paper by following the broken line, open out the paper and you have a complete head gusset. The length of the underbody gusset is measured from C to D as indicated by arrows on the outline shape of the horse. As the outline shown has the slimmer shape of a racehorse, the gusset is started lower at C. If it was a carthorse, where a broad chest is required, the underbody gusset would be measured from A at the throat to D. The underbody gusset, which controls the width of the toy in its widest part should measure three-quarters of the body pattern, indicated on the outline at G–H. To give an example: if the measurement C–D is 35.5cm (14in) and three-quarters the width G–H is 10.3cm (4in), then a piece of tracing paper is required 35.5 x 10.3cm (14in long x 4in wide). Fold it in half lengthways, lay it on the body pattern and lift the paper at each end as indicated, which produces folds where shown on the diagram.

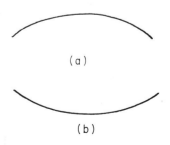

DIAGRAM 37 Underbody gusset shaping. (a) An upward curve produces a fat toy. (b) A downward curve produces a slim toy

47

Draw round the body outline as shown by broken lines; the curves at the legs are for darting. Cut away excess paper following the broken lines, open out the tracing paper and you have designed the underbody gusset. Interest can be added to a toy by making the legs attain different positions, for example in a running form. People are sometimes wary of diverging from the basic straight standing toy. All that is required with the change in stature is the underbody designed and cut to match.

NECK ON A RAG DOLL

A two-piece head pattern can sometimes cause wrinkling at the neck of the doll. To avoid this happening use a continuous head gusset starting at the shoulder, up the side of the neck, round and across the head, down the other side of the neck and to the opposite shoulder. To design this gusset to the correct size fold a piece of paper lengthways and lay this parallel to the shoulder on the silhouette pattern. Turn the paper continuously so that it follows the line of the head pattern and each time the paper is turned at that exact spot make a point on both the paper and the pattern. Continue until the top centre of the head is reached. This provides half the gusset length, so when cutting out the full gusset place this pattern piece onto the fold of the material. Should the design of your doll require an alteration in the gusset width, then adjust accordingly; however, a gusset of an equal width the full length is acceptable.

A seam joining head and body of a rag doll at the neck will also prevent wrinkling. Support can be given by covered dowelling, and neck darts can be useful.

Body proportions

The younger the figure the larger the head in relation to the body. As the figure becomes older the legs and arms become longer in relation to the length of the body. These facts have to be taken into consideration when designing figures which are required to be authentic and balanced. Diagram 38 provides some body pattern shapes for rag doll designs.

DIAGRAM 38 Rag doll body pattern shapes

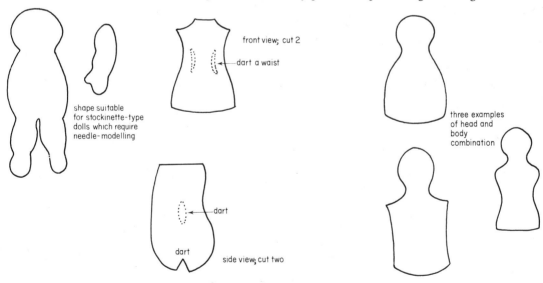

shape suitable for stockinette-type dolls which require needle-modelling

front view; cut 2

dart a waist

dart

dart

side view; cut two

three examples of head and body combination

DARTING

A gusset can produce bulk; a dart can control this bulk, or add localised shaping in small areas. Large darting will not compensate for poor shaping in the original design. Darts are often used at the top of the head, for example on a bear where broadness is required. The diagrams will show areas which are often darted. On a rag doll if a half dart (curve) is put where the arm is placed on the back of the body and an inward curve

Jack-in-the-box

Asleep two-faced doll

Awake two-faced doll

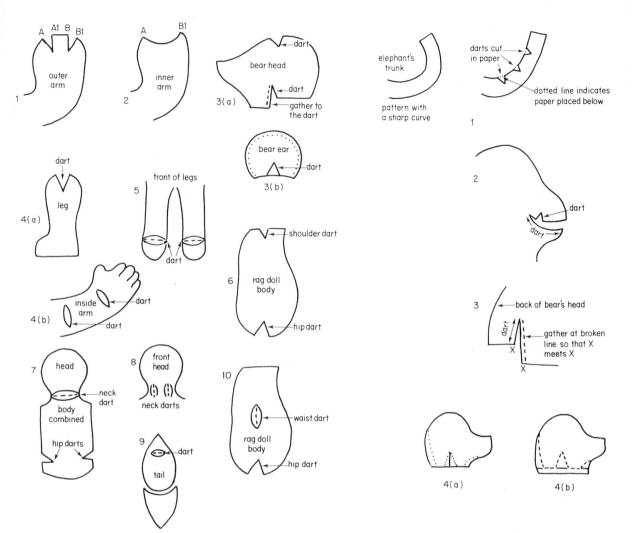

DIAGRAM 39 Use of darts. **1.** Darting on the outer arm skin to add fullness. **2.** No darting as the limb is required to lay flat to the body. This inner arm **2** matches the outer arm **1.** **3 (a).** Darting at the top of the head makes the shaping pronounced and widens the head. At the base of the head combined gathering and darting produces a cheek and also widens the head. **3 (b).** Darting to shape the ear. **4 (a).** Darting at the top of an outer leg skin adds fullness to the limb. **4 (b).** Darting on the inside arm pattern piece to bring the arm round towards the body for a baby doll. On

the matching half of the limb there is no darting. **5.** Darting used at the front of the legs to turn up and shape the foot. **6.** Darting at the top of the body to assist shoulder formation. Darting at the body base to produce hip shaping. **7.** Darting at the neck to prevent neck wobble on a combined body and head pattern. Dart should be inwards. A dart also produces hip shaping. **8.** Darting at the neck to add shaping to a flat doll. **9.** Darting at the tail tip to turn the tail tip and add interest to the shape. **10.** Darting to produce a waist. Dart inwards. Dart at the body base to produce hip shaping

DIAGRAM 40 Darting a pattern. **1.** Where a pattern has a sharp curve, darts cut in the paper pattern will produce a gentler curve. Lay the pattern onto another piece of paper and glue to hold. Re-cut the new pattern shape. **2.** Adding a dart to form a rounded cheek. The smaller dart is incorporated in a larger dart. **3.** Darting at the back of a bear's head to add shaping. **4 (a).** When adding a dart to give roundness to a head it will pull in the skin where indicated by a dotted line and this will produce a slim outline. To compensate for this darting add width to the outline of pattern **4 (b)**

added to the front arm pattern, this brings the arm forward. These curves must be outward ones on the back body and on the back piece of the arm to correspond, and inward curves on the front body and arm pattern.

Similarly, a half dart (curve) on a front leg piece at the ankle will bring the foot forward without curving it upwards and a reverse dart curve will produce a heel in the foot.

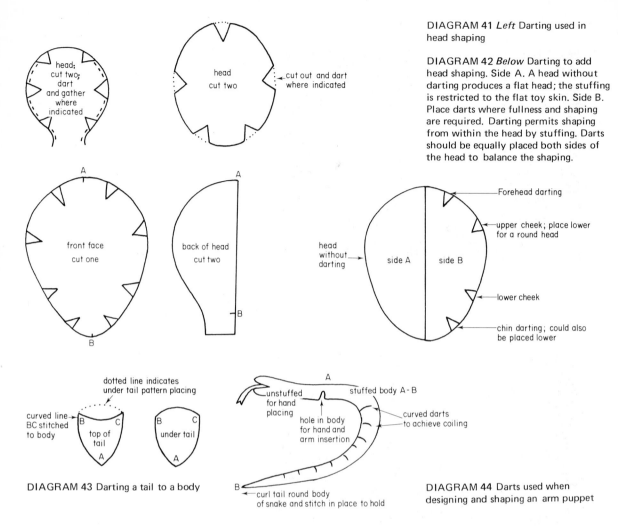

DIAGRAM 41 *Left* Darting used in head shaping

DIAGRAM 42 *Below* Darting to add head shaping. Side A. A head without darting produces a flat head; the stuffing is restricted to the flat toy skin. Side B. Place darts where fullness and shaping are required. Darting permits shaping from within the head by stuffing. Darts should be equally placed both sides of the head to balance the shaping.

head: cut two; dart and gather where indicated

head cut two

cut out and dart where indicated

A

front face cut one

B

A

back of head cut two

B

head without darting

side A side B

Forehead darting

upper cheek; place lower for a round head

lower cheek

chin darting; could also be placed lower

dotted line indicates under tail pattern placing

curved line BC stitched to body

B   C

top of tail

A

B   C

under tail

A

DIAGRAM 43 Darting a tail to a body

A

unstuffed for hand placing

hole in body for hand and arm insertion

stuffed body A-B

curved darts to achieve coiling

B

curl tail round body of snake and stitch in place to hold

DIAGRAM 44 Darts used when designing and shaping an arm puppet

THE USE OF GATHERING

Gathering in toy design should be used in moderation; consider the shaping element first. However, it can be a very useful method for achieving fullness with a limb, face or body. If the gathering line on the top outside of a leg piece is placed to produce fullness to the outer part of the limb only, then the inside of the limb must be made smaller to match the reduced size which the outer gathering will produce.

If fullness is required at a jaw line, take into account the way the gathered piece will fit into the toy outline. It can be a good policy to break the face into separate construction pieces with the gathered part made as a section of a side face panel.

CONSTRUCTION OF A TOY SKIN

The soft toy animal in its most basic form has the limbs incorporated in the outline of the toy. Progressing further, limbs are ladder stitched onto the body after the body and limbs have been stuffed with toy filling. There are other ways of constructing a toy skin which will be illustrated.

Adding limbs together at skin construction stage

Circles can be cut out of the inner arm and inner leg of the toy. Corresponding circles are cut in the body where the limbs should be placed. The toy skin is stitched together, then turned to the right side and is left, at this

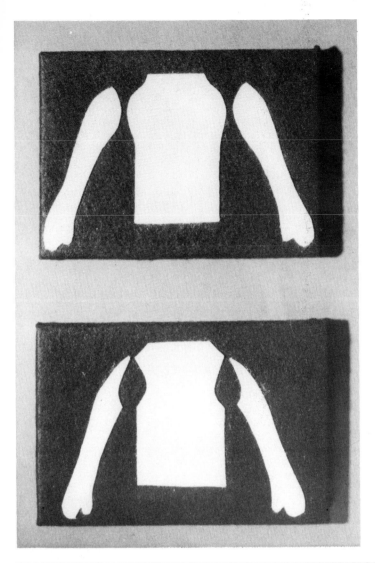

10. Points to note in pattern construction: half darts. The top pattern shows the back body and arm pieces, the bottom pattern the front body and arm pieces

11. Darting on leg pieces

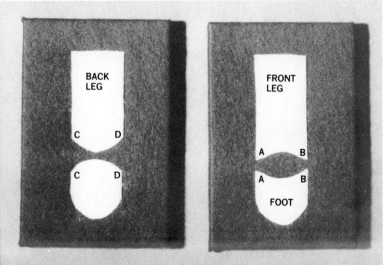

BACK
LEG

C   D

C   D

FRONT
LEG

A   B

A   B

FOOT

stage, unstuffed. The limbs are stitched, then turned to the right side and also left without toy filling. The cut-out circle on the inner arm is then matched up to the cut-out circle on the body at arm position. From within the body pin both cut-out circles together, i.e. arm and body circles, then backstitch round to secure the circles together. Treat the other arm and the legs likewise. Stuff the limbs first. Finally stuff the body. This method is very useful for attaching wings to ducks, especially if on a small scale.

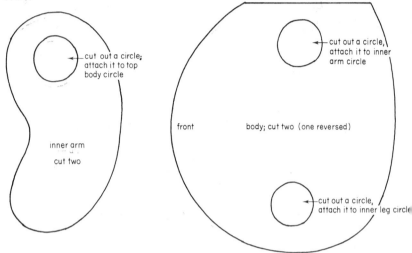

DIAGRAM 45 Attaching limbs by cut out circles

Construction of limbs within the toy skin design

This is a more difficult process and one which the toymaker will progress to as knowledge is gained. It will assist in the building towards this expertise to study other designers' pattern shapes achieved in the finished toy. After a while you will notice that you begin to criticise certain patterns and see how they could be improved; when this stage is reached you are well on the way to becoming a toy designer. The shaping of the body of the toy is such that the shaped limbs can be stitched in place as part of the toy skin. Likewise when applying pads to toys they can be ladder stitched in place after the toy is made up and stuffed; the diagram shows how the pad can be constructed as part of the toy skin prior to stitching the arm pieces together.

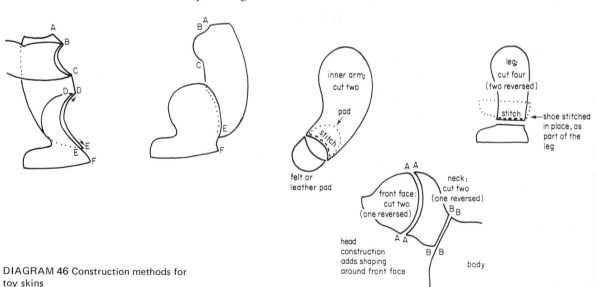

DIAGRAM 46 Construction methods for toy skins

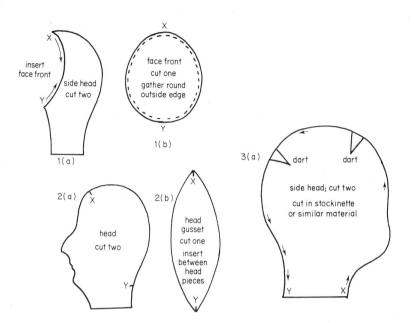

insert face front

side head
cut two

1(a)

X

face front
cut one
gather round
outside edge

1(b)

X

Y

2(a)

X

head
cut two

Y

2(b)

X

head
gusset
cut one

insert
between
head
pieces

Y

3(a)

dart   dart

side head; cut two

cut in stockinette
or similar material

Y   X

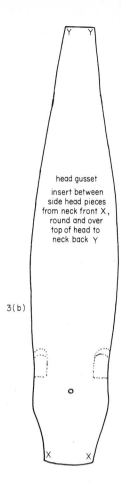

head gusset

insert between
side head pieces
from neck front X,
round and over
top of head to
neck back Y

3(b)

Y Y

X X

The profile head

A cloth head with well-defined features can be made by drawing an outline shape with strong features. Cut out the outline twice in fabric and stitch
both pieces together. The line down the centre of the face may be rather
unsightly unless it is to be for, say, a witch. To hide the seam on the head
after stuffing cover it with a stretchy material — nylon or stockinette.
This forms a complete 'skin' and where necessary can be needle-modelled.

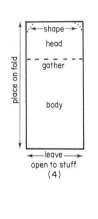

shape

head

gather

body

place on fold

leave
open to stuff
(4)

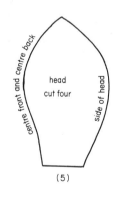

centre front and centre back

head
cut four

side of head

(5)

face front;
cut one

dart where
indicated

6(a)

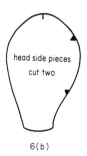

head side pieces
cut two

6(b)

DIAGRAMS 47 & 48 Head pattern
designs

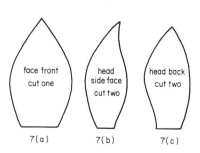

face front
cut one

7(a)

head
side face
cut two

7(b)

head back
cut two

7(c)

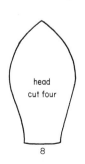

head
cut four

8

CONTOURING AND SCULPTING ON A RAG DOLL FACE

When designing a rag doll it is possible to shape and build up the face so that it becomes an exciting design concept. Most rag dolls tend to have flat faces and one imagines that this can be the only medium for rag dolls unless one is using a moulded felt mask, needle-modelling or carefully darting and stuffing with toy filling. Another process will be explained here which leads to creating dolls which have great individuality.

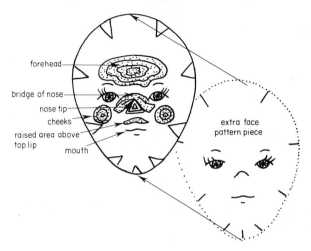

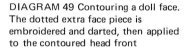

DIAGRAM 49 Contouring a doll face. The dotted extra face piece is embroidered and darted, then applied to the contoured head front

Firstly, it is essential to use a head design which has adequate darting in the forehead, chin and cheek areas. Both felt and firm cotton materials are suitable for this method. Cut out the pattern pieces — i.e. head, body, arms and legs — plus an extra front face piece slightly larger all round than the original pattern. Make and stuff the doll, and using a soft pencil draw on the features, keeping a tracing of the features to draw or embroider a duplicate set of features on the extra face piece. Dart the extra face piece as on the made-up doll. The contouring is done by cutting out pieces of felt or thin foam sheeting, and building them onto the stuffed head to produce contours so that when the extra face piece is applied over it, feature shaping is the result.

As a guide to which places to build up, use a mirror and constantly refer to your own face. Areas which may require building up are across the forehead, nose, cheeks, top of lip, and chin. The felt pieces must start small and build up in size so that when the larger piece is laid over the smaller pieces it completely masks them. If you start with large pieces building up to the smaller pieces, not only would unsightly ridges form but the raised areas would form hollows in the top face skin. The diagram suggests suitable shapes to use. To secure felt pieces to the face use pins until you are satisfied with the results, then glue to hold. About four layers is usually sufficient, depending on how pronounced the contouring required is. After building up the felt pieces place the extra face piece over them and pin it in place. When satisfied that the contouring is as required, the extra front face piece can be stitched and the pins removed.

A similar process to the laminating of a doll mask can be used with contouring. After the felt contours have been glued to hold, paint the whole of the stuffed head face surface with glue and lay over the extra felt face piece; pin, then stitch to hold, and press with the tips of your fingers on the face to shape and sculpture it. This sculpturing must be done whilst the glue is still moist. It will dry hard as in the lamination method.

Margaret Hutchings, in her book *Dolls and How to Make Them*, describes the process of painting a cloth doll to make a hard surface. This led to my experimenting not only with paints but also various glues, for it seemed feasible that if felt soaked in glue, moulded and then dried, became a useful medium when making laminated masks, then doll faces and bodies could be painted after contouring to produce a Lenci-type finish. (For a description of the Lenci process refer to the section on laminating and mask materials.) Liquid white glue was the most successful. Apply it in thin layers all over the face, allowing each layer to dry completely before applying the next coat. You will find that it will gradually start to look like transparent wax. This opens a potential development area for designing dolls linked to historical designs.

DESIGNING MINIATURE TOYS
It is a completely wrong assumption that a small toy is an easier starting point than a larger one; whatever the size of the toymaker's hands they will not alter to the scale of the toy. A good practice in dealing with miniature designs is to make the pattern larger than required at first. Make the toy, overcome any difficulties, then scale the pattern down to the required smaller version; having made it once should help considerably. To make miniature toys the designer must think small in every way. Use small tools, for example tweezers, cocktail sticks, etc. Toy fillings must be lightweight, like Kapok, which has a fine texture and can easily be pushed into the smaller areas. Sewing thread and needle must also be fine, the thread blending with the fabric. The texture of hair is most important; embroidery threads and crepe hair are very useful. Materials for dressing must be lightweight and preferably the types which do not fray. Raw edges of woven fabrics can be sealed to prevent fraying by spreading with glue on the wrong side. The patterns on materials must be small. Any accessories must be to the same scale as the toy, and toys in groups or as part of a scene must be scaled in relation to each item. Once the habit of thinking small has been formed the problems which at first seemed insurmountable disappear, and the toymaker begins to watch at all times for the opportunity to obtain miniature articles — narrow ribbons, tiny artificial flowers, etc.

ARMATURE SHAPES
When designing figures or dolls for a display group project or a doll's house there are a variety of ways of constructing the basic figures.

Corset lace dolls
These are made by cutting lengths of corset lace and threading them with pipe cleaners. This makes them bendable and easy to position. The ends of the lace are glued and cut into hand or foot shapes. The feet must be weighted; dressmaking weights are suitable provided the toy is not for a young child. Cover the feet with felt cut in the shape of shoes. To simulate stockings or socks bind the base of the leg with cotton or thread. The head is a circle of material gathered round the outside edge and stuffed firmly; the gathering is then pulled tightly and fastened off. This ball head is applied to the top of the corset lace body. These dolls can be dressed and then bent into the required shapes.

Wired figures
These have an armature wire shape which can be bound in the same way as when wiring a toy — see the section in the previous chapter. The wires are constructed into a basic figure shape covered with tape to bind it together. The figure shape can then be built up with toy filling and bound with strips of sheeting. The head is made by a gathered circle front section stitched to two half-head pieces cut for the back of the head. Wire-framed figures make excellent string puppets; each limb section is wired to the next — for example, the lower leg to the upper leg. Each part is packed with stuffing and bound, each join being left free for easy moving.

UTILISING A PATTERN TO ITS FULLEST POTENTIAL
Designing can be time consuming, and in the case of a rather stylised toy

12. Double-ended awake/asleep rabbit,
showing both ends of the rabbit and
the double skirt

13. *Below* Awake rabbit. Asleep rabbit
end is hidden under the skirt of the dress

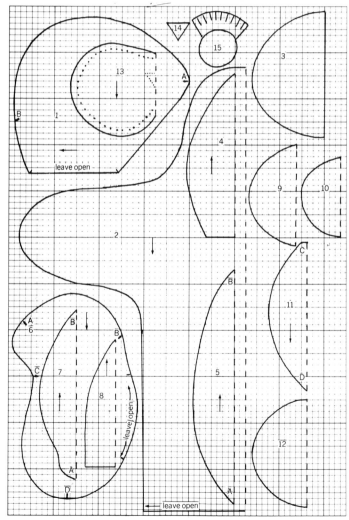

the time spent is rewarded by an end product which is very special. Designs of a more basic nature, however, can be expoited in a variety of ways. To illustrate this I will take the example of a rabbit pattern I used. With very few adaptations it became a wide range of different toys, the head being the original design used for all the following toys. By explaining the development of each it should help you to relate, and find the potential, in your own designs.

First the head. This is a basic construction of two side head pieces, and the shape was copied from a drawing of a rabbit. The head required width at the top and so a head gusset was added. The ears were constructed as given in Chapter 7. Eyes, nose and whiskers completed the features. A baby rabbit was also designed.

The head was added to a basic puppet glove and this became the Jack-in-the-box rabbit. (See Chapter 10.)

By adding the top body part of a rag doll and arms (plus a duplicate set) this became the basis for the awake/asleep double-ended toy.

The head added to a glove body, with the addition of legs and adapting a bought basket as a perambulator, produced the puppet with a baby rabbit and perambulator set.

By enlarging the head pattern and adding extra pieces of fur fabric for mouth shaping plus a tooth, and the body and limbs construction of gathered fur circles, this became the circle rabbit toy.

Using the top halves of the body and head as for the double ended rabbit, and placing these constructions into a bed, an attractive night-dress case was made.

14. The perambulator is a bought basket with wooden wheels added and a hood comprising a strip of material, hemmed both sides, with covered wire inserted through the front hem and secured into the basket sides; the back hem is gathered tightly

DIAGRAM 50 *Left* Rabbit pattern. **1–5**. Puppet and Jack in the box. **1**. Head. **2**. Glove body. **3**. Tail. (Form a circle half body colour, half white). **4**. Ear. **5**. Head gusset. **6–12**. Baby rabbit. **6**. Body. **7**. Head gusset. **8**. Ear. **9**. Foot. **10**. Paw. **11**. Stomach gusset. **12**. Tail. **13–15**. Fur circle rabbit. Puppet head enlarged plus: **13**. Muzzle piece. **14**. Nose. **15**. Eye back.

N.B. All broken lines indicate 'on fold' of material. This pattern demonstrates the expansion of a pattern and does not therefore include making instructions. However, pile lines, annotations and accompanying photographs will enable the reader to construct the rabbits if they wish, or they can adapt the pattern to their particular toy requirements

The rabbit glove puppet secured to a wooden spoon inserted into a felt top hat became a stick puppet.

The baby rabbits with ribbons attached to the top of their heads became a hanging pram toy. Half the body cut in fur fabric and appliquéd to a fur fabric pram blanket makes an attractive matching pram set.

These ideas developed very easily and naturally from the original designs. This book will enable you to progress even further with this theme. The straw hat and basket plus other accessories can go to dress the finished rabbits. Design other heads and apply them to the ideas given. If you are producing toys commercially or as a cottage industry it can be very boring to produce the same toy day after day. Possibly the need to make sufficient toys to meet placed orders may make further designing impossible. By extending the uses of the pattern as described it adds variety for the toymaker, makes ordering of materials fairly easy and gives a range of samples to offer the toy purchaser.

A point to mention here is that many toy pattern outline shapes can be very useful as templates for designing animal or toy collages for a child's bedroom. Cut out in fur fabric and attractive prints they can be appliquéd to a felt or material backing chosen to match or complement the colour scheme of the room — a very original item. Sectional balls may require appliquéd shapes; again, pattern shapes already available are useful without the need for additional designing.

15. Fur circle rabbit

16. Fur fabric pram cover. Appliquéd rabbits and stuffed duplicate pattern rabbits made to match as hanging toys

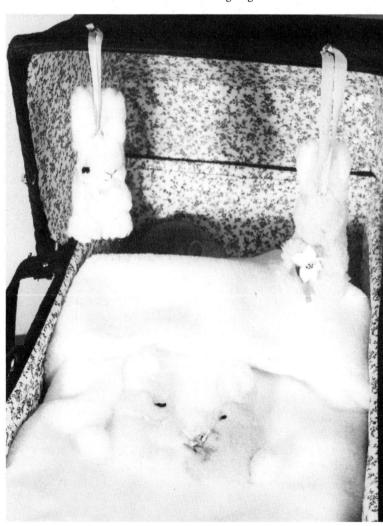

THE APPROACH AND METHODS TO DESIGNING
A SPECIFIC TOY SUBJECT

Example: Clowns

First research the basic history of the subject; only with facts can you approach the actual designing with knowledge to add authenticity to the toy.

Clowns were in being thousands of years ago; a danga, a wild-looking creature, entertained the Pharoah of Egypt over four thousand years ago. The jester was the fool and the clown at court. Modern clowns have much of the jester's make-up, costume and character. The jester often carried a marotte; this was a short staff, at one end of which was carved a jester's head. The jester used this marotte as a puppet. The clown or joey was named after Joseph Grimaldi, the famous clown. The true clown derives from the white-face pierrot character of the Commedia Dell 'Arte but owes much of his spangled costume to the character of Harlequin. Pierrot is the white costumed, white faced, sad clown derived from the original Pedrolino of the Commedia Dell 'Arte, a mime Clown. Harlequin was also an original character from the Commedia Dell 'Arte. He wore a chequered costume which started out as a costume covered in patches which later became triangles of red, blue and green divided by thin yellow braid. Later, spangles were added. He usually wears a black mask and sometimes a black skull cap.

The Auguste first appeared in Elizabethan times in the person of Richard Tarleton, a Shakespearian actor. The Auguste wears exaggerated versions of everyday dress. These clothes can either be brightly coloured or of dull colours as a tramp might dress. The make-up is also exaggerated and usually consists of large red noses and a happy or sad expression. Most circus Augustes are referred to as clowns when in fact a clown is, as stated already, a white faced person in a brightly coloured costume covered in spangles. An interesting fact relating to the clown's make-up: a Mr Bult who resided in Surrey, England, designed clown faces which he painted on goose eggs. These eggs he sold for one guinea to clowns and this make-up then became the exclusive property of the clown.

How to proceed

Once you have some basic facts and some sketches there is sufficient information and material to start designing the subject. Obviously if you are intending to design to a level where all the toy must be authentic then the research of the individual subject must be to a greater depth.

CONCLUSION

So much is trial and error and a toymaker certainly learns by successes and failures. One important fact all students of the craft should bear in mind is the importance of enjoying toymaking. I have held some classes where students have produced most attractive toys that have employed very few design principles. Toy designers are to be admired for their artistic work, but I hope toymakers will always view the pleasure of their creation taking precedence over their design principles, and let their own creativity come to the fore.

Anne Dyer, a craft author, once wrote in a book she gave me, "Beware, toys look like their makers." I have found this to be absolutely correct. Sometimes I have had fifteen students in a class all using the same toy pattern and every toy will be a little different, with maybe a slight change of expression, stuffing or the placing of the eyes. It is, of course completely different when each student designs their own toys; thin students tend to design thin toys and vice versa!

6 Processes which may provide a useful extension to soft toy techniques

PLASTER OF PARIS

Paris was built on a large area of gypsum deposits, and so the name plaster of Paris was derived, although gypsum is found all over the world. Plaster of Paris was introduced into England by Henry III because he was so impressed by the superb quality of French plaster work.

General process

Plaster, when added to water, soon hardens, and if you wish to increase the speed of the hardening use hot water instead of cold or add alum to the water. To slow the hardening process barely mix the water and plaster or add several teaspoons of vinegar to the water. Plaster must be kept in a dry place because it soon becomes unusable if stored in a damp atmosphere or on a damp floor. Always add plaster to water; never the other way round, and use one part plaster to two to three parts water; only half fill the bowl, and you will find plastic easier to clean. Sprinkle the dry plaster onto the surface and continue until the level of the plaster reaches the surface of the water. Leave for about two minutes, then mix well trying to avoid making any bubbles. Work quickly as the plaster starts hardening rapidly. The mixture must be poured into your moulds whilst the mixture is still thin. To be of the correct consistency to use with scrim/muslin on armatures it must have the appearance of thick cream. If it becomes crumbly it is of no further use. Casts and moulds become very warm whilst reaching setting point. Never wash out your used bowls in the sink as the plaster will set in the drains.

Making a cast from plaster of Paris

Materials: A cardboard or plastic tray, thin enough to tear away once the cast is set. Depth approximately 1.3cm (½in) deeper at sides than height of model when lying in tray.
Plaster of Paris.

Method 1: Mix plaster of Paris with water; coat the bottom of the tray. Lay the model which has previously been greased face down. Pour in more plaster to the half-way mark. Mark your head with a pencil at the half-way mark; this makes it easier to see when to stop pouring the plaster. Set aside to harden. Grease the flat plaster edge completely. Mix more plaster and completely cover the head. Leave to set, then remove from the container. Mark a few indentations in the two moulds so that you can match up the two halves. This cast is excellent to use for moulding papier mâché.

Method 2. Materials: Plasticine or clay. Plaster of Paris. Roll out plasticine or clay; press an object into it. Before pouring in the mixed plaster into this impression a wall must be pressed firmly to the base to contain the plaster; plasticine or clay is suitable. If the cast is over 30.5cm (12in) in diameter it is advisable to add a layer of scrim/muslin to the plaster to strengthen it. Leave plaster to harden and then remove the retaining wall. Remove the plasticine or clay from the plaster. If a few pieces adhere to the plaster, wash the next day to remove.

Method 3. Making a face or head in plasticine. Materials: Plasticine. To make a face or head cast, mould the head in plasticine by kneading and shaping into a ball shape. When moulding the original head in plasticine it is essential to ensure the outside edges are straight, so that when the plasticine model is cut in half and the mould made the two halves of the plaster cast will match up. The plasticine mould can be cut crossways as illustrated, or down the centre of the head from top of head to base of neck.

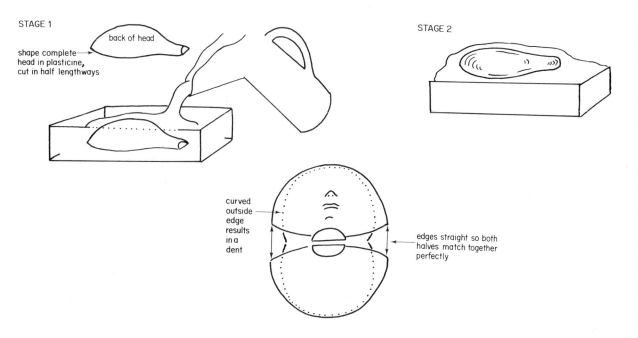

STAGE 1

back of head

shape complete head in plasticine, cut in half lengthways

STAGE 2

curved outside edge results in a dent

edges straight so both halves match together perfectly

PLASTIC WOOD

Excellent for moulding a head in a cast. It is rather difficult to work with, and care must be taken that no air bubbles occur between the plastic wood and the mould or cast. It must be well pressed into the mould. It is light in weight and is a useful material to use.

PAPIER MACHE

Papier mâché craft first began in China and then spread in to Japan, Burma, India and Persia. These countries still produce articles in papier mâché to a very high standard. Papier mâché was used in several countries for doll making in the eighteenth and nineteenth centuries. The first patent taken out in America for a doll with a papier mâché head was in 1858, the work of Ludwig Greiner. (The first time baby dolls were made in this medium was in Germany in 1850). In the 1870s Philip Goldsmith ran a retail store in Covington, Kentucky, and together with other merchandise he also sold dolls. With a man called Wolf Fletcher he experimented with a papier mâché doll, the head of which was made of flour, glue and paper pulp. The bodies were constructed in cloth material and stuffed. The head was dipped in flesh-coloured paint and the cheeks coloured. After this two coats of clear varnish were applied.

Papier mâché is very versatile. It is used extensively at carnival time when huge figures are made. Papier mâché can be made in the form of pulp or of layers of paper glued together to cover existing objects, for free modelling and for moulding. Materials are inexpensive. You need newspapers, wallpaper and wheat paste (for example, Polycell or Glutas) and galvanised wire or chicken wire for the armatures of various models. Various paper types can be used for making papier mâché, and whilst the basic methods are similar, different combinations can be used.

DIAGRAM 51 Making a mould. Stage 1: Place the mould into a box approximately 1.3 cm (½ in) deeper than the height of the mould. Mix the plaster of Paris and pour it over the mould, completely covering it. To assist the easy removal of the mould from the cast paint it all over with soapy water prior to pouring on the plaster. Stage 2: Allow the plaster to set. Turn the box upside down and tear away the sides. A hollow cast remains of the head back to use for future modelling. Treat the front of the head in the same way.

Method 1
Materials: Newspaper, Polycell paste.

Tear newspaper into small pieces and soak in a bucket of warm water. Do not cut the newspaper as this prolongs the time needed for the paper to disintegrate; tearing the paper helps the fibres to loosen in the warm water. Leave to soak overnight, then mash with a stick. Take handfuls of the paper and squeeze out as much water as possible. Break the damp pulp into crumbs and either sprinkle dry paste into it or add mixed Polycell. Mix thoroughly into the crumbs. When fully mixed it is ready to use.

A point to note is that when you are using newspaper for your pulp the print comes off onto your hands. Wait until you have finished handling it and then wash your hands, and the print will come away easily. If you wash during the process you remove some of the natural oils in your skin, and the newsprint really stains and is then difficult to remove.

Method 2
Materials: Porous cardboard egg boxes, Polycell paste.

Break the egg boxes into small pieces and place into a basin. Ideally the texture should almost be to powder form. Cover with the water. Leave to soak well until all the water can be squeezed out and the mixture remaining can be pressed into a ball and retains its shape. Mix the Polycell paste and stir well until it thickens. Break the drained egg box material mixture into the glue, and stir well until it is completely integrated.

Method 3
Materials: Tissue paper, Polycell paste.

As for Method 1. Tissue paper is a more expensive material than newspaper for papier mâché, but it produces moulds of a much finer quality. It is for the toymaker to decide which material is most suitable for the required end product.

Method 4
Particularly suitable for a solid modelled head.
Materials: Newspaper, cellulose paste, plastic filler.

Shred newspaper into small pieces. Boil the shredded newspaper for half to three-quarters of an hour with a small quantity of water until mixed. Stir to prevent burning. Add more water and shredded paper during boiling as necessary. Leave pulp to cool. Drain through a colander to remove any excess water. To this mixture add the cellulose paste and plastic filler. Quantity will vary according to the pulp; as a rough guide 35 large sheets of newspaper produce 200g (7oz) of pulp. Add to this quantity approximately 28g (1oz) of cellulose paste and add only a small amount of water to mix. Mix all together thoroughly. Mould the article and leave to dry. Smooth away any excess roughness with a fine grade glasspaper. Paint the base with emulsion paint. Add the features by whatever medium chosen.

Fixing a head to a cloth body
(a) Set a hook into the neck prior to the papier mâché drying, or . . .
(b) model your head round a base stick or support.

Method 5
The consistency of this pulp enables it to be used exactly as modelling clay.
Materials: Pastel paper or newspaper, whiting, glue, flour paste.

Tear the paper into small shreds no larger than 2.5cm (1in) square. Soak overnight in water. Pour off the water and beat the paper to a pulp until free of lumps. Remove water by squeezing thoroughly. Two sheets of newspaper makes a ball of pulp just smaller than the size of a tennis ball. Add to this two dessertspoons of whiting and enough flour paste to make the mixture the correct consistency for modelling. Model as if for clay and leave to harden. Sand and paint as for method 4. This pulp can be cast in a mould to make, for example, a limb. Alternatively a mould can be made of plaster or modelling clay (method 2, plaster of Paris) by pressing clay on a doll's body. The pulp is pressed into the mould, then left to dry. The mould is then cut away. This papier mâché mixture has a finer surface than ordinary papier mâché. An even finer coat can be achieved by two or three coats of gesso.

Finally paint with egg tempera or cryla colours. (Cryla colours are acrylic paints – *U.S.* Liquitex.).

Method 6
To cover a mould.
Materials: Newspaper, vaseline or plastic cling-wrap, Polycell paste.

To cover a mould first protect it with vaseline or plastic cling-wrap. Tear strips of newspaper and dip into the mixed paste. Remove the excess paste by gently pulling the paper between two fingers. Lay the soaked strips of paper onto the mould, completely covering it. Apply a second layer as before, this time laying at 45° from the first. Continue to change the angle each time until five or six layers have been applied. As you progress with adding the soaked paper pieces press them well into the models features; patience at this stage will be rewarded. If the article requires extra support add a layer of muslin which has been previously soaked in a mixture of white P.V.A. glue and plaster of Paris. Leave in a dry, warm place to set.

Gently prise the mask away from its base model. If you completely covered the base mould it will be necessary to cut across the head from side to side with a sharp craft knife. This will enable the removal of the two halves, which can then be stuck together either with strong glue or self-adhesive tape. If the inside of the mask needs further strengthening add tissue or white paper soaked in paste as for previous applications. Keep the moisture content low and be careful not to spoil any features. Leave to dry. If you only made a half mask you will require a back section. This can be a solid pulp head, a cast made from papier mâché, or plasticine head, a stuffed fabric head or a stiffened fabric head. It is advisable to leave free the outside edge of any fabric, without soaking, for sewing.

Method 7
Materials: Newspaper, glue, sawdust, plaster of Paris, washing soda.

Soak small pieces of newspaper thoroughly in hot water, adding a teaspoon of washing soda. Stir in a cupful of sawdust and boil until pulped. Leave to cool. Add the glue powder and plaster of Paris until the consistency is suitable for modelling. Form an egg-shaped head. Insert a piece of dowelling to hold the head whilst being moulded. The hole made by the dowelling is used to insert the neck once the head is set and dried. The hollow neck is glued in place.

POWDERED PAPIER MACHE
Available from craft shops. Carefully follow the instructions; it tends to cause dust. Once mixed with water it is excellent for modelling either by casting or direct modelling. Due to the head being solid it is rather heavy.

HOLLOW HEAD
You may require a hollow head to reduce the weight. Fill a material head base either with sawdust or cat litter granules. The bag is then closed at the base by tying with cord or string and securing it to a stand. Model over this base bag with papier mâché. The sawdust or cat litter will absorb the moisture and this aids quick drying. The base string can be undone when the model is dry which will release the sawdust or litter granules and the bag can then be removed and re-used. The model will require a final drying after the removal of the bag and contents.

STAND TO ENABLE EASY MOULDING OF HEAD

When moulding a head it is essential to have complete freedom of movement for both hands and the model must be stable. Whilst it is easy to fill an empty wine bottle with sand and mould on top of this, if you are making a number of heads it is useful to have a purpose built stand. The photograph shows a stand design which enables the moulding of up to four heads at a time. The dowelling supports vary in size so choice can be made according to the project being modelled. Space has been allowed between each dowelling upright to cater for projects requiring breastplates. This stand is also useful for holding fabric heads whilst painting features.

17. Stand to enable the easy moulding of heads

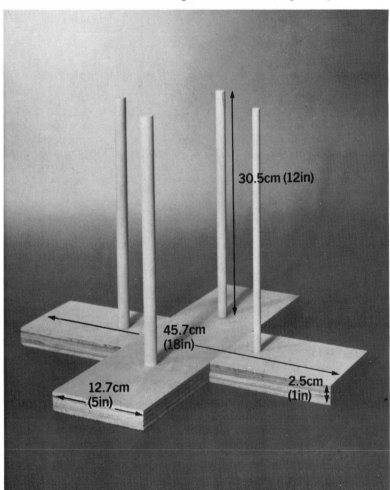

BREASTPLATE AND HEAD COMBINATION

To form a breast plate add an oblong of cardboard to the top of the dowel rod before the headpiece is applied. Apply the base of the headpiece to meet the cardboard and proceed to work the head and breastplate, moulding them together, using one of the papier mâché methods best suited to the project. (No. 6 is a particularly suitable method.) This model can then be completely covered with a base coat of emulsion paint, and the features added by whatever medium is required. To add durability to the model apply one coat of matt varnish; this will seal the base paint. For most projects this treatment is sufficient. However, should you be repairing an old model or requiring a very good quality finish, this can be achieved by polishing the model with a good quality transparent wax polish.

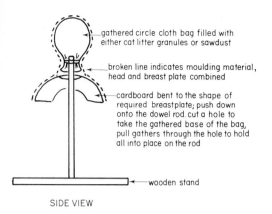

gathered circle cloth bag filled with either cat litter granules or sawdust

broken line indicates moulding material, head and breast plate combined

cardboard bent to the shape of required breastplate; push down onto the dowel rod. cut a hole to take the gathered base of the bag, pull gathers through the hole to hold all into place on the rod

wooden stand

SIDE VIEW

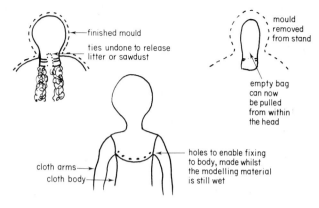

finished mould

ties undone to release litter or sawdust

mould removed from stand

empty bag can now be pulled from within the head

cloth arms
cloth body

holes to enable fixing to body, made whilst the modelling material is still wet

FRONT VIEW

DIAGRAM 52 Moulding a head and breastplate

LAMINATED PAPIER MACHE

Particularly suitable for breastplate and head combination.

Materials

Tissue paper, flour paste of a thick consistency.

Method

Grease the object with vaseline or face cream. Cut the tissue into small pieces. Dip these into the paste and apply to the model, overlapping well until the base is fully covered. Repeat this process until you have built up six to eight layers of soaked tissue. It is of assistance to ensure full coverage if more than one colour tissue is used. Smooth at each stage as you progress to ensure any joins are invisible. Dry thoroughly. (An airing cupboard is ideal.) Rub the surface smooth after drying as it will have developed wrinkles. To obtain a really fine surface a few thin layers of gesso may be applied.

This method produces a mask of a much more delicate nature than the laminated felt method.

THE INSERTION OF A MODELLED HAND INTO A CLOTH ARM

Using the diagram as a guide, place the hand inside the sleeve, with the right side of the sleeve inside. Bind the sleeve to the wrist of the modelled hand with wire, or strong cord. Bring the sleeve back over the hand to cover the wrist. The wire holds the sleeve and wrist secure. It assists the retention of the material to the hand if during the modelling of the hand either a ridge or an indentation (flange) is made round the wrist.

LAMINATING AND MASK MATERIALS

Mrs Izannah Walker of Central Falls, America, was one of the first people to consider producing rag dolls commercially. For the faces she stiffened the face fabric with glue, reinforced this with layers of webbing, then stuffed it. Although she used this method for many years it was not until 1873 that she decided to apply for a patent.

Much later, in 1924, Chad Valley of England took out a patent for a doll's head made partially or wholly of textiles or felt stiffened with shellac or starch. In Italy in 1921 the Lenci Doll Company started making felt dolls which were stiffened and machine pressed to manufacture the faces. Later the bodies were also of pressed, stiffened cloth.

First choose a pattern of a body you may already have, and find a head to fit, i.e. with the same proportion. If you are successful at designing you will experience no difficulty in designing a body to fit any head size.

The choice of the doll's head on which to mould your mask is a comparatively easy task. You may have a suitable head on a treasured old

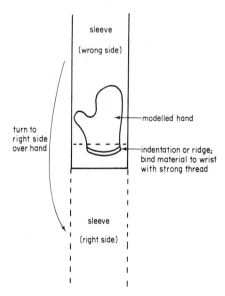

sleeve
(wrong side)

turn to right side over hand

modelled hand

indentation or ridge; bind material to wrist with strong thread

sleeve
(right side)

DIAGRAM 53 The insertion of a modelled hand in a cloth arm

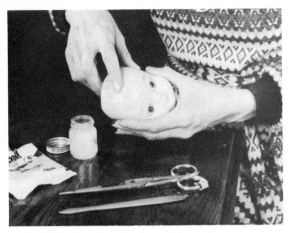

18(a). Laminating. Greasing the mould

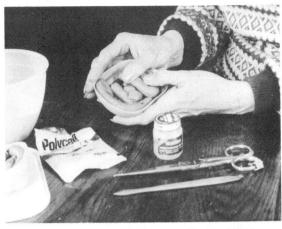

18(b). Filling a mould with plasticine to retain shape whilst laminating

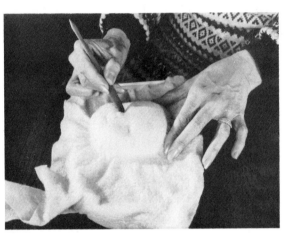

18(c). Laying felt, previously soaked in paste, over the mould and pressing to shape

18(d). Testing the mould to see if it is completely dry

18(e). Removing dried masking material from the mould. Vaseline has enabled easy removal. This mould was covered with scrim prior to applying the felt

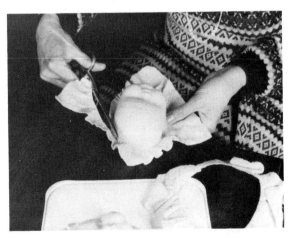

18(f). Trimming excess material

doll. Doll masks are available at a small cost and are of a more superior design of recent times than the previous rather stiff characters. Jumble sales are often ideal venues for obtaining broken dolls which may still have their head intact. If preferred you may mould your head as already described earlier in clay or plasticine. The main consideration is that the model has well-pronounced features, because to a certain extent the 'strength' of the features is reduced in the final end product.

Method

Having chosen your mould, grease it thoroughly with vaseline, this is to prevent the masking material sticking to the mould. When making a mould on a commercially made plastic hollow mask it is desirable to fill it with plaster or plasticine to give it extra stability. One alternative is to imbed it in a ball of plasticine to hold it steady. Make sure it is not twisted or distorted in any way.

Measure mould and cut out your chosen material layer combination large enough to cover the mould completely.

Using mixed polycell paste soak the materials thoroughly. Some felts of rather a thick quality do not absorb the paste easily. In this case soak it for a while in water before wringing it out and putting it into the paste. *Note:* always lay the materials on the greased mould on the diagonal.

Taking your first material layer, squeeze it out to remove excess paste. Lay over the mould and press the material well into the feature. Treat further layers likewise. A knitting needle, cocktail stick or modelling tool is useful to assist the pressing of the materials into the indentations of features on the mould.

Place the covered mould in a warm place to dry slowly. During this drying time occasionally press the materials back into the feature indentations. When completely dry remove from the mould and trim excess material to a good shape. (Later I describe the processes of fixing a mask to a previously made doll's head.)

Designing the Back of a Head for a Laminated Mask

Measure the head sideways. Reverse the head. Draw the back of the head to fit. Two halves are required for the back head pattern. Slightly curve the pattern on the dotted line to fit the face. Dart the neck if it has become too large in the designing. To join the two pieces of the back of the head, stitch the curve on both pieces to the seam on the face. Stuff it firmly to support the features. Ladder stitch down the back of the head

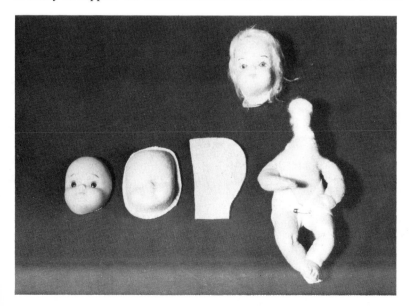

19. Laminating. *Left to right:* model used as a mould; laminated mask; felt head back pieces to be applied to the mask; stuffed laminated head with hair applied and painted features; wired felt body, needle-modelled to provide dimpling at knees, wrists and elbows. The top of the body wire is inserted into the head which is then stitched to the body

DIAGRAM 54 *Below* Methods of designing the back of a head for a rag doll pattern. Suitable for use with a manufactured doll mask, and for a laminated mask

DIAGRAM 55 *Right* An alternative method is to attach a mask to a cloth ball head

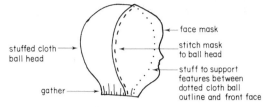

ALTERNATIVE METHOD. MASK ATTACHED TO A CLOTH BALL HEAD

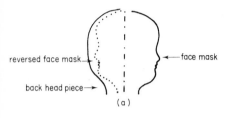

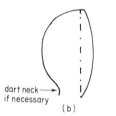

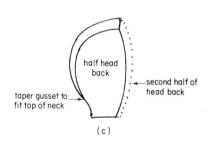

to seam it together. For a large doll it may be necessary to insert a gusset between the two back head pieces. Taper the gusset into the top of the neck. For a three-piece back of head insert the gusset and leave one curved side piece open to stuff, then ladder stitch to close the opening.

LAMINATING: MATERIAL COMBINATIONS

FIRST LAYER	SECOND LAYER	TOP LAYER
White buckram; with glue this gives strength and shape to the mask.	An inter-layer to hide the rather coarse buckram mesh. Muslin is suitable.	Final layer to resemble skin. The material must be a fine texture, for example silk, crêpe or nylon.
Paper soaked in Polycell paste and wrung out. Carefully moulded to the model's features.	Muslin soaked in Polycell paste and wrung out.	Felt soaked in Polycell paste and wrung out.
Muslin, soaked in Polycell paste.	Muslin, soaked in Polycell paste.	Felt, soaked in Polycell paste and wrung out.
Muslin, soaked in Polycell paste.		Stockinette soaked in Polycell paste.

Grease all moulds prior to applying the material layers. Dry all masks thoroughly, then prise off from the moulds and make a back head. Laminating can also be used for moulding toy hats. A circle of felt is soaked in Polycell secured over the top of a container with an elastic band. If a smooth brim is needed, cut off the shaped brim and stitch on a circle of felt with the centre removed to the crown.

Modelling material

When making limbs for an old-fashioned doll which may consist of a fabric body with porcelain effect head, arms and legs, an excellent modelling material to use is Fimo. Originating in Germany it is now widely stocked. Fimo is available in many attractive colours but the transparent block No. 01 is the best choice for dollmaking to the above requirements. Fimo must be kneaded well to make it really pliable. It is then modelled and placed on aluminium foil in a preheated oven not hotter, in the case of the transparent material, than 99°C (210°F), to harden. This should take about 20–25 minutes; do not exceed this time. The models are then removed and left to cool. The next stage is the careful painting of the features; it is then coated with acrylic lacquer. A doll wig to complement the subject is then glued to the head, and the limbs attached to the cloth body as already described. Fimo is a pleasant material to work with and is non-toxic.

7 Features and characteristics

If you are making a realistic animal, look up in an encyclopaedia the facts on, for example, the position of the eyes, size and shape of the mouth, etc. If the subject is a rag doll type or a toy with a character, cut out paper shapes of the features and pin them onto the face to see the effect. Go away and leave it for a while, then come back. If you are not satisfied with the result, move them around to obtain the best effect or the one required.

EYES

Whilst a toy is often without a nose or mouth, it rarely appears without eyes! It is surprising how the eyes are always the main feature; they are the key to the face.

The British Standard Code of Safety requires that plastic safety-lock eyes in stuffed toys should be able to be attached to a 23kg (50lb) weight and still remain in the toy. Before inserting safety-lock eyes stuff the toy lightly so that the exact position of the eyes can be gauged and marked.

plastic eye front — eye shank
metal washer — pushed right down on eye shank flat to eye back
fur fabric of toy skin

DIAGRAM 56 Cross section of safety-lock eye in position

Remove the stuffing, insert the eyes and stuff the head firmly. If you fail to do this it can completely change the head shape and the eyes will be in the wrong place. This happens particularly with toys which have a snout. If the above procedure is not observed you can end up with a toy with eyes near the ears, and the whole expression of the toy is spoilt because bears look more attractive with eyes well down towards the snout.

Never trust the place marked for the eye on a pattern; the toy may have altered shape in the sewing process. Use the mark as a guide only and alter to suit the toy. Eyes placed low on a snout give a young expression; if placed closely together they immediately create a sly expression.

A brief guide to the position of eyes: human eyes are half-way on a line with the centre of the face; animals eyes are usually half-way between nose and ears (closer to nose to look younger); hunted animals always look sideways; reptiles have pale centres to their eyes; pig's eyes are at an angle. Features placed low on the face of a doll leaving a high forehead produces a young expression. The higher features get on a face the older the subject becomes. A face without hair should be divided into thirds for an adult toy and halves for a baby doll toy.

Plastic safety-lcok eyes

Plastic safety-lock eyes, the type with press on backs, are very suitable for toys requiring to look realistic. These eyes are available in a variety of sizes, colours and pupil shapes. They comprise two parts, the plastic eye and the metal washer. They are often supplied with a plastic tool, which is a dome plastic piece with one end left open. Having decided on the eye position, make a small hole in the position on the toy skin with the point of a pair of scissors. Push the eye shank through the hole from the right side of the toy to the inside. Lay the toy with the inserted eye onto a covered soft surface; foam rubber is excellent as it does not slip. Turn the skin of the toy back so that the shank of the eye is exposed. With the curved outer edge of the metal washer facing away from the eye, push this washer onto the eye shank with the curved dome by banging the dome

DIAGRAM 57 Eyes. **1.** Felt circles with stranded embroidery thread eye lashes. **2.** Embroidered iris, pupil and lashes, white felt eye base. **3.** Felt and embroidered eye lashes. **4.** Felt combination plus embroidered lashes. **5.** Embroidered in backstitch as outlining. **6.** Embroidered. **7.** The iris of the eye is embroidered as the spokes of a wheel from the centre with a single strand of embroidery thread. The pupil is in black satin stitch using two strands of embroidery thread. **8.** Suitable for a clown. **9.** Indian. **10.** Chinese. **11.** Felt circle, embroidered eye lashes. **12.** Two felt circles, one light, one dark. **13.** Satin stitch embroidered circle. **14.** Button with embroidered eye lashes. Only suitable for stylized eyes for subjects intended for teenagers and adults

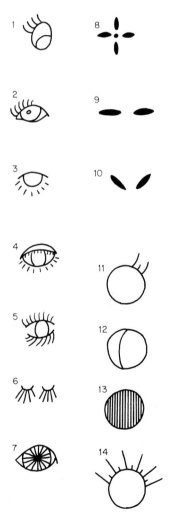

sharply with a hammer. If no tool is available a cotton reel can be used with the paper end covering removed. The cotton-reel hole is placed over the washer and the eye shank is hit with a hammer, which pushes the washer flat to the toy skin and eye back. There are also safety-lock eyes available where the metal washer is much thinner and can easily be pressed on by hand. This type has a washer which is flat round the edge, not curved. These are quite safe, simply a slightly different design. If the fur fabric has a knitted back it may run once the hole is made for the eye shank. To rectify this glue a piece of felt or material behind the place where the insertion is to come; this will add support. If, after placing the eye, it is discovered it is not well placed, the only way to remove it is to cut the washer with wire cutters or, in the case of the thinner washer, to lever it off with a screwdriver. It is then necessary to repair the hole, if it is not too large, by gathering with tiny stitches and pulling tightly at the back. If, however, the hole is large, it is better to sew a patch of the same fur fabric onto the back. If this is not satisfactory it may be necessary to use one of the other types of eyes described, for example a combination felt one.

Embroidered eyes

If a more pronounced eye on a toy is required to add character, embroidery can be the answer. First, onto a circle of soft white material, draw an eye shape and embroider it with embroidery thread. (The material should be larger all round than the eye size required). Gather the outside edge and either place a domed button or stuff it very firmly (the latter if it is for a very young child), then gather up firmly and sew this tightly into place on the toy. If in doubt go round a second time. If it is a fur toy make sure the eye is well embedded into the fur to give a more realistic effect.

If the eyes are being embroidered straight onto a rag doll's face it is better to do this before finally stuffing the toy. However, do as described earlier to find the exact spot for the eyes by lightly stuffing and marking the eye spot; then remove the stuffing and embroider the eyes.

Novelty eyes

Goggle eyes are white plastic circles with clear plastic fronts, with an enclosed movable black circle. As the toy is moved the black circles move to give expression. At one time these were only available as sew-on eyes with a back similar to a button. Now they are available with white plastic screw-on backs. If you are a toymaker get into the habit of looking out for materials, trimmings, wools or novelty strip, evening-dress-type trimming or sequins. Eyes can be made most attractively by combining materials with sequins or beads sewn in the centre. This looks particularly successful on a clown or animated toy.

Felt eyes

This is probably one of the most effective ways of portraying characters, whatever the toy subject. Small felt circles can be cut with a leather punch, with paper backing the felt. Larger circles will need drawing pins of different sizes. First put a drawing pin into felt and draw or cut round this outside edge; this is much more accurate than cutting a circle and laying this on to felt to cut round as the second cutting is always larger. It is better to sew on a felt eye to avoid the child picking it off the toy; however, there are occasions when a glued eye is required and in these cases always use Copydex. Ordinary adhesives only stick to the fluffy surface of the felt and can be pulled off easily; Copydex soaks into the felt and secures the eye firmly.

Plastic or glass eyes can have their colour altered by placing a circle or oblong of felt in a different or deeper shade behind the eye before fixing the metal back, in this order: eye, felt, fur or fabric of toy, and metal eye back washer securing all. Felt circles behind eyes of bears cut 1.3cm (½in) in larger all round can look most attractive, and are useful if you wish the eye to look larger. Always cut the felt sufficiently large to allow a certain shrinkage when the metal washer pulls the eye tightly, which in turn pulls on the felt; if there is not sufficient allowance round the edge, the felt can well disappear altogether behind the eye when the washer is fixed.

If eye lids are not being added, cut down the size of the eyes at the top of the eyes where lids would be — this avoids a staring effect to the eye.

In working out colour combinations for felt eyes, always use the darkest colour in the centre. If using a light colour in the middle for a special reason keep it as small as possible to avoid a hypnotic effect. A felt eye is often built up from a combination of felt circles of differing sizes. First decide on the size of the finished eye and cut out a circle to correspond with this. Usually this largest circle is the palest colour, often white. On to this add a smaller circle, usually a colour to blend with the toy. Add to this the third circle, which is the darkest colour. The eye at this stage can look very dead, so a highlight is necessary to add sparkle and light.

Either add the highlight low on the dark circle in a tiny pyramid at A or higher, at B, if the whole eye is dark add the highlight at C. The eye is now ready to be ladder stitched onto the toy. As with an embroidered eye make sure it is well embedded; if the eye looks a little flat, before finally completing the sewing of it to the toy add a little stuffing between the eye and toy skin. Felt eyes are not washable.

Make sure the running stitch on the outside of a round eye which is to be protruding is small and neat to avoid a ridged edge which would occur if stitches were large.

FELT EYE

ADDING HIGHLIGHTS

DIAGRAM 58 (a) Eyes

Eyelids

Cut a circle of felt in half to make two eyelids; stick eyelashes along the bottom straight edge or, if using felt lashes, sew them along the edge of the lid. Cut out two more complete circles the same size as the first one and place a safety-lock eye in the centre. If using felt eyes glue these onto the circle. Glue the top half of the eye to the centre of the lid, gather round the top circle and pull it behind the eye to make an outline. If you require two felt lids (an upper and lower as in some animals) do the same process as described but place a lower lid as well as upper one.

DIAGRAM 58 (b) Eyelid

if eye lids are not being added cut down the eye size at the top where the lids would normally be; this reduces the staring effect

  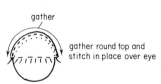

cut felt circle in half

sew or glue eyelashes in place

gather

gather round top and stitch in place over eye

False eyelashes

False eyelashes from chemists are very useful if toymaking; it is not necessary to purchase expensive ones. Care must be taken when applying them. For example, if using them with an embroidered eye use a fine paintbrush to apply a thin line of glue just above the eyelid; apply a thin line of glue on the lashes and position them as naturally as possible on the doll. Trim as required. If applying lashes to painted eyes carefully test first that the glue will not make the paint run.

eyelashes combined with the eye construction by sewing A–B

DIAGRAM 59 Various eyelash constructions. With the macramé method the eyelashes are either glued to the top of the eye or under the eyelid

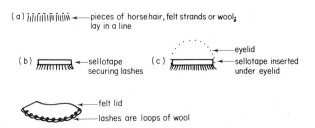

(a) pieces of horsehair, felt strands or wool; lay in a line

(b) sellotape securing lashes

(c) eyelid — sellotape inserted under eyelid

felt lid — lashes are loops of wool

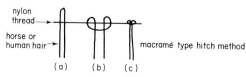

nylon thread

horse or human hair

macramé type hitch method

(a) (b) (c)

DIAGRAM 60 Eyebrows

Eyebrows

Always blend them with the hair and complexion colouring. Black lines on a doll or model face can look very harsh and are really only suitable for dramatic make-up requirements. If you add a small quantity of blue to the black before applying to the face, this softens it considerably.

EARS

Avoid human ears; cover where they should be with hair. It is rare to use ears on a rag doll. Animal ears must look realistic. Put a small pleat 0.7cm (¼in) to 1.3cm (½in) in the base of the ear to save bulging. Always stiffen large ears if they are required to stand erect or they will become limp and floppy. For difficult placings start sewing in the centre and work out to one edge, doing the same for the other half of the ear. This ensures a firm hold with no weakness at the edge. Animal ears should always be put on in a curve or folded, never pulled straight. If in doubt as to the position of ears consult a picture of the animal and be guided by the real thing.

Ears can be stiffened with pipe cleaners, bound wire or a lining of Vilene. Always cut the lining 0.7cm (¼in) smaller for a fabric such as felt, or if using fur fabric as ear lining cut out 1.3cm (½in) smaller than the ear pattern; this pulls the outside edge into a curl and gives a more realistic and natural shape.

Even when ears are well wired or stiffened they can still fall towards the outside of the head; it is then necessary to add some bracing stitches. In the event of the ears flopping when they are meant to be erect, take a needle and strong thread, secure it firmly to the inside base of an ear, take the needle and thread through the stuffed head to the inside of the other ear, pull firmly and pass through the head again to finish off where you started. Do not pull so hard that you squeeze the head out of shape; provided the head was well stuffed in the first instance this should not happen, as a well-stuffed head acts as a support to pull the ears against. (This method can also be used for spindly legs, in fact anywhere on a toy where you have two limbs that can be supported by pulling on each other, with threads in between, and passed through the body.) Whilst a toy is sometimes greatly improved with a little bracing here and there in parts already mentioned, it cannot compensate for poor stuffing, but can only achieve a finished look to shape.

Method of applying ears

Ears on a fur fabric toy animal can either be inserted into a slit in the head or ladder stitched on afterwards.

Method 1: inserting an ear into a slit

Sew round the outside edge of the ear. Turn to the right side and oversew the open edge. Insert the ear into the slit previously cut according to the pattern until the oversewn edge of the ear is approximately 0.7cm (¼in) from the pattern outline. Stitch the ear to one edge, then sew it onto the opposite side of the slit. When turned to the right side – if the pattern was accurate – the ear will be in the correct place. The head can then be stuffed. With some patterns it is necessary to line the oversewn edge of the ear level with the toy outline and oversew all together.

Method 2: applying an ear by ladder stitching

This method is preferable as it is easier to obtain a more realistic look to the toy. Prepare the ear as for method 1. Then, using coloured headed pins, secure the ear in place on the stuffed toy head. Ladder stitch to hold, forming a natural curve, stitching both the front and back of the ear. Apply other ear to match.

Bear ear

Stitch with right sides facing. Turn to right side. Overstitch raw edges A–B using strong thread. Before fastening off pull gently on A–B to gather

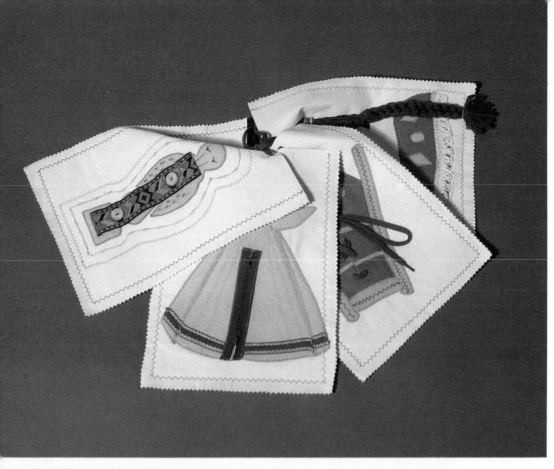

Rag book

Jack-in-the-box puppet

Rabbit nightdress case

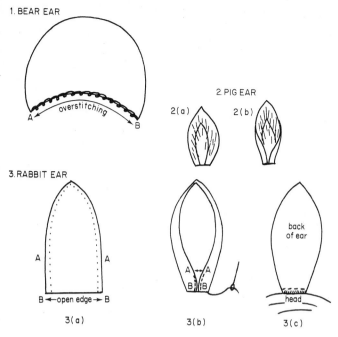

1. BEAR EAR

overstitching

A   B

2. PIG EAR

2(a)   2(b)

3. RABBIT EAR

A   A

B ← open edge → B

3(a)

A → A

B   B

3(b)

back
of ear

head

3(c)

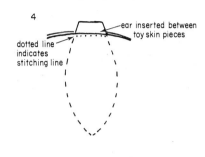

DIAGRAM 61 Ears. **1**. bear, **2**. pig, **3**. rabbit. **4**. Shows the insertion of an ear between the toy head skin pieces

4

ear inserted between
toy skin pieces

dotted line
indicates
stitching line

and form a natural curve. Fasten to hold at B. Do not detach the thread but use it to attach the ear to the head by ladder stitching.

Pig ear
2(a) Add ear lining and simulate hair using either stitches in horse hair or fine thread.
2(b) Ear completely folded and stitched at the base as for rabbit ears.

Rabbit ear
3(a) Fur fabric rabbit ear. Dotted line indicates the placing of the felt ear lining.
3(b) Fold B to B. Stitch from A—A to hold the fold. Bring the thread out at the corner of the ear base. Overstitch the bottom edge as for the bear's ear.
3(c) When ladder stitching the back of the ear to the head, tuck in the shaded area and stitch slightly higher to pull the ear into an upright position. Firmly ladder stitch all round the ear base to apply to the head.

NOSES
It is not necessary to put noses on rag dolls or a pretty feminine face; sometimes two tiny beige French knots are all that is required, or a tiny circle of felt. Some noses can add greatly to a comedy character like a clown. If a nose is required refer to the contouring method.

When making and stitching circular noses, do first make sure the running stitches round the outside of the circle of material are very small and near together. If you are making large stitches it may save time at the running stitch stage but will add to the difficulty when sewing the nose on. After sewing small stitches pull up the circle and stuff. Pull tightly after stuffing to make a nice firm knob and put a few stitches to stop the gathering unwinding. Place the nose onto the face of the toy and start to ladder stitch; continue right round the nose and if necessary go round a second time. If the stitches had been large they would have formed large ridges round the nose when gathered and these would get in the way when sewing on the nose. Small stitches in the first place almost eliminate the ridges and are so much easier to cope with.

If you find it difficult to make a nose on an animal that really looks

• two french knots

METHOD 1. Embroidered

METHOD 3. Folded felt

o small felt circle

METHOD 2. Folded felt

X   Z
X .... Z
cut one in felt

METHOD 4. Felt covered card

O felt oval

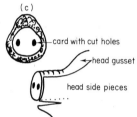
card

⌣ tiny embroidered curve

METHOD 5. Snout
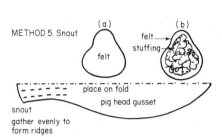
(a) (b) (c)
felt
felt→
stuffing
place on fold
pig head gusset
snout
gather evenly to
form ridges
card with cut holes
head gusset
head side pieces

O felt circle

DIAGRAM 62 Noses

DIAGRAM 63 Noses. Method 1.
Embroidered. Stitch across first, then
stitch from top to bottom of the nose.
Method 2. Match X—X and Z—Z; this
folds the felt to form nostrils. Method
3. Match A—B on one side and A—B on
the other side. Pin, then stitch. Ladder
stitch nose to the toy and add an
embroidered mouth with stranded
embroidery cotton. Method 4. Lay a
piece of card onto felt. Stitch around
the outside edge and gather to fit the
card. Fasten off. Ladder stitch to the

toy, with the gathering facing the fur
fabric skin and the plain felt surface
to the front. Inbed the nose as you
stitch into the fur fabric. Method 5.
Gather the head gusset snout evenly
to form ridges. Insert the gusset into
the head sides. Apply the prepared
snout — see diagrams **(a), (b)** and **(c)**
— into the head where indicated with
ladder stitches. Stitch through felt
and nostril holes and pull on the thread
to needle-model. Secure to hold. Stuff
snout firmly

STAGE 1
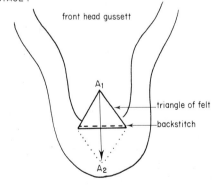
front head gussett
A_1
triangle of felt
backstitch
A_2

STAGE 2
front head gusset
C B
A
C B
A

DIAGRAM 64 Attaching a felt nose
to a bear. Stage 1. Place triangle of
felt with point facing upwards. Stitch
small backstitches at base on the wrong
side. Bring A_1 down to A_2. Stage 2.
Ladder stitch B to A and C to A. Then
stitch side to side to pull the nose into

shape. Stitch into any folds or crinkles
on the edge of the felt; this will remove
them and produce a tailored nose. The
small diagram shows the direction of
the stitching to remove any crinkles
after ladder stitching

right — it can go wrong in the stuffing and fixing — try this method. Copy the shape of the nose required, trace this onto a piece of card, then cut a piece of felt approximately 0.7cm (¼in) larger all round than the cardboard. Either glue or sew this on the card and secure at the back making sure the front is smooth. Sew this felt-covered nose shape to the toy with ladder stitching.

Also available on the market are pre-moulded noses with a shank and washer on same principle as for safety-lock eyes.

On a bear, felt can make a satisfactory nose. If you have any oddments of suede or leather these can transform an ordinary animal into one of an exceptionally good standard. A really healthy animal has a shiny nose, so why not add this feature to a toy animal? Cut a circle of satin material or one with a shiny surface, sew all round the outside edge with a neat running stitch, gather then push the circle flat and sew onto the nose point. The more unusual reptiles, animals and crocodiles have nostrils. In the case of a dragon, where it may be necessary to produce the effect of fire breathing, they immediately become a necessary feature.

SNOUT OR BEAKS
These can be made with 0.7cm (¼in), 1.3cm (½in) or full circles. The fuller the circle the wider the cone is at base and the less sharp the point.

So often a toy can be spoiled by sewing the beak on afterwards. If it is meant to be a real life toy, the beak very seldom looks part of the bird if applied in that way. However, look at the pattern carefully and see if you can use the following method. (This can also be used for applying legs and feet on a bird.)

20. Swan's beak

DIAGRAM 65 **(a)** Three piece beaks 65 **(b)** Cut circles produce various beak sizes 65 **(c)** Inserting a beak 65 **(d)** Construction for a swan's beak

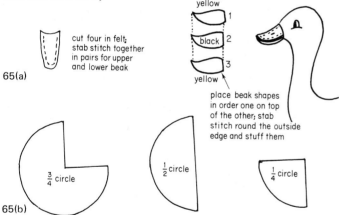

cut four in felt; stab stitch together in pairs for upper and lower beak

65(a)

yellow
1
black
2
3
yellow

place beak shapes in order one on top of the other; stab stitch round the outside edge and stuff them

¾ circle

½ circle

¼ circle

65(b)

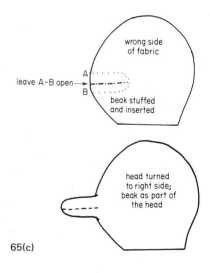

wrong side of fabric

A
leave A–B open→
B

beak stuffed and inserted

head turned to right side; beak as part of the head

65(c)

Leave open a small piece the same width as circle on beak A–B. Insert the stuffed beak right side uppermost inside the head (which is still inside out) with the edges of the beak level with the edges of the mouth A–B. Back stitch all round this circle making sure to leave a circle. Finish off firmly, then turn to the right side and the beak can then be popped to the outside. Stuff the head very firmly; when reaching the opening of the beak inside the head make sure the stuffing is firm round the opening. Leaving a gap between the stuffing in the beak and the head will cause the beak to droop. (The same process can be used for applying the feet and wings of birds.)

MOUTHS
For a human mouth use different shades for top and bottom lips, always a darker tone at the bottom. Use pale shades of pink for female characters, brown for males; never use red unless for clowns or character figures — it is far too harsh. A slight curve upwards will produce a smiling, happy expression. When embroidering the nose on teddy bears always add an embroidered mouth.

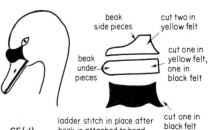

beak side pieces
cut two in yellow felt

beak under-pieces
cut one in yellow felt, one in black felt

ladder stitch in place after beak is attached to head
cut one in black felt

65(d)

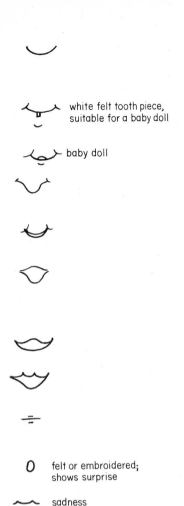

white felt tooth piece, suitable for a baby doll

baby doll

top curves embroidered in a lighter tone than the bottom piece

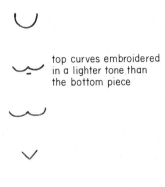

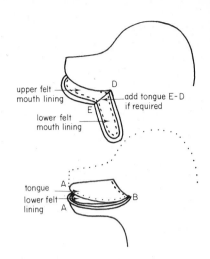

DIAGRAM 66 Embroidered mouths

DIAGRAM 67 Inserting a mouth piece

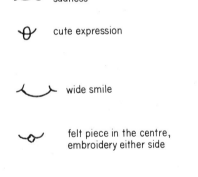

O felt or embroidered; shows surprise

sadness

cute expression

wide smile

felt piece in the centre, embroidery either side

Open mouth

If requiring a bear to have an open mouth, cut into the pattern below the mouth. Cut an oblong of pink felt and either point or curve each end. (See diagram 67.) The size of the oblong is determined by the amount the mouth is to open. Measure ABA; allow for opening. This will determine the inner mouth size. If the process proves to be difficult to attempt from the inside of the toy it is possible to work from the outside of the toy, ladder stitching the inner mouth to head.

TEETH
See diagram.

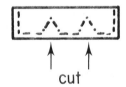

 cut

DIAGRAM 68 Teeth. When making felt teeth, for example for a rabbit, it is easier to stitch first and then cut afterwards

CHEEKS

Circles of felt can be added as cheeks on a rag doll, either as a plain circle, or embroidered over and through a circle with embroidery thread like a wheel. Choose a slightly darker tone felt to the face material, a deeper pink cheek on a pale pink face, or for a peachy tone face choose a deeper peach cheek. So often people immediately think of pink when making the skin of a rag doll, when it would look so much nicer in peach- or flesh-coloured materials. Pinks tend to look much brighter when made up. To make a really elegant doll pay careful attention to colour tones; a cream flesh goes well with brown or russet hair, with a small print fabric for a dress in brown or green. An apron, if added, should be in cream. For dolls dressed in blues use a pale flesh colour for skin and dark hair. (Cheeks can be coloured by fabric crayons etc.)

DIAGRAM 69 Cheeks. **(a)** Felt circle to tone with the doll colouring. Darker beige on a cream skin doll. Pink tones on a flesh coloured skin. **(b)** Felt circle with stranded embroidery thread worked over it to secure to the doll face. The thread should shade in with the felt and toy skin. **(c)** Embroidered directly onto the toy cheek with stranded embroidery thread

(a)   (b)   (c)

FRECKLES

Freckles on a toy can be enchanting, and add such character if used in moderation. Ideally put just a few around the bridge of the nose area; even though they are small, do pay attention to the colouring. If the toy's hair is ginger, use a cream face and add ginger freckles; if brown, use the various beige tones available for freckles. These are done in embroidered French knots. Freckles can also be applied using fabric crayons and paints.

COLOURING FEATURES

There are various mediums for colouring the features on toys. Fabric dyes are developing and making it possible for the toymaker to experiment and use plain materials to design very exciting effects. Embroidery and application of felt features are often preferable methods, but colouring agents may enable an otherwise impossible special effect to be created.

Lipstick

This must be carefully added. Bear in mind you can add more but cannot take away, so use it sparingly. Dab lipstick onto the required spot, then put a piece of clean rag over this place and gently iron with a warm iron over the spot; this will seal it.

Food colouring

(Cochineal etc.) This can be used satisfactorily; first lightly wet the area where the colouring is required, then carefully apply the colouring with a soft paintbrush; again, use sparingly. The colour will spread, so only wet as far as the colour is to go.

Wax crayons

Test the wax crayons on a scrap of the material being used, for colour suitability. When applied to the toy, iron to seal it using a clean rag as described above.

Fabric printing dyes

The features can be painted directly on to the cloth by using a mixture of Dylon Paint and Dylon Cold Dye. Paint thickens the dye so that it can be applied with a brush. This method is suitable for cotton, linen and soft leather. Rowney fabric painting dye is another liquid paint which is suitable for cotton, linen and some synthetic materials.

Fabric crayons

Finart Fabricrayons are a useful medium for the toymaker. The features are drawn onto paper, then laid face down on the fabric as you might use a transfer. A warm iron is passed over the layers which transfer the design onto the fabric; the heat fixes the dyes. Crayon dyes are very useful for synthetic fabrics.

Nail polishes

Provided these are well applied they can be most effective and are a useful way to use up unwanted colours.

Indian ink

Useful for the pupils of a rag doll's eyes, although black thread is more commonly used.

Face powder

Any type is suitable, whether loose or cream compacted. This can produce a nice soft blush to a rag doll's cheeks.

Oil photographic colours

These are excellent; as with the other methods mentioned practise well before applying to the model.

Water colours

Use artist's, not student's, quality because the student's type are synthetic. Water colours mixed with white emulsion can produce desired colours for painting a mask.

Emulsion paint

Use to paint over a papier mâché model after it has completely dried.

Acrylic paint

This can be added in a skin tone after the emulsion paint has dried. This is quick drying. Coloured acrylic paint added to white acrylic paint can be diluted with a little water, then applied.

Brushes

Oil brushes sizes 4, 6, 8 are ideal for mask base coat. Sable, sizes 1, 4, 8, for the finer delicate addition of features.

Tinting with tea

Skin can be coloured either by dying the cloth with bought dyes or using cold tea. This can be tinted to a pinker tone with a small quantity of pink dye. Add only a few drops at a time as it is too easy to end up with raspberry-coloured material!

Wax polish

To obtain a translucent effect to a finished mask apply clear wax polish and buff thoroughly with a soft cloth.

Painting eyes

To provide a good base it is advisable to use white enamel the day previous to painting the face. Then apply the iris; this must dry before the pupil is painted. Add highlights when the eye combination is fully dry to give depth to the eye expression. A small pale pink dot at each end of the eye corners adds realism.

Painting faces

When choosing mask-making materials consider the expression required and the colouring medium best suited to achieve the desired effect. Coarse textured materials may prove difficult if the object is to achieve a delicate finish, and a smoother material may be more suitable.

Hot water dyes

Dylon multi-purpose dyes. Mix ½ teaspoon dye powder to a paste with some cold water. Add ½l (1pt) of boiling water, then 2l (4pt) of hot water. Put in the cloth and bring to simmering point; gradually add 1½ teaspoons of salt. Simmer 20 mins at 194°F (90°C). Use on cotton, linen, rayon, nylon and terylene.
ICI Chlorazol direct dyes. Mix 1 teaspoon of dye powder to paste with cold water. Add ½l (1pt) of boiling water. Add 2l (4pt) of water, and keep the dye liquid simmering for 20 mins; 3 teaspoons of salt should be added gradually. Use on cotton and linen and viscose rayon.

Cold water dyes

Dissolve 1 small tin of dye (or 2½ teaspoons) in ½l (1pt) of warm water. Stir well. Dissolve 4 tablespoons of salt and 1 tablespoon soda in ½l (1pt) hot water. Stir well and cool. When the cloth is ready for dyeing, mix the two solutions together. The cloth should be wet before it is immersed in the dye. Dye for ½ to 1 hour. Stir from time to time while the material is in the dye. Rinse the material well in cold water, until the water runs clear. Cover with boiling water, add detergent, and leave for 5 mins. Wash and dry.

HAIR

Do not restrict yourself to using wool; different materials can add great fun and character to a toy. The following materials are suitable, but consider carefully the toy's character, the safety factors and the use of the toy: lampshade fringe, net, striped material, fur fabric, brushed nylon strand, beads, frayed out tweed material, frayed hessian, lampshade bobble braid, embroidery threads, crepe hair, old knitted jumpers cut up to produce small woollen curls, knitting and crochet yarn — loosely crocheted chain stitch produces excellent hair, some nylon mixture yarns which have a sheen to them which is ideal for Asian dolls. Raffia is useful, but only on dolls which have a fixed hair style, for example a scarecrow. Many toy component firms supply excellent dolls' wigs. Mohair (nylon wigging) is often available from chemists or hairdressers dealing in theatrical supplies. (See the end section for addresses.)

70(a)

70(b)

Colour

It is most important to consider carefully the colour choice for hair. Complement the complexion of the doll. Unless making a clown character, avoid colours which are too strong.

Balance

It is most important to balance the weight and quantity of hair in relation to the size of the toy. Too much hair is as bad as too little where bald patches show through.

Styling methods

Ringlets are formed by twisting together several strands of wool then, still holding the twist lightly, folding the length in half so that it twists round itself. Stitch the ends securely to the head, hidden under the hair.

For short curls, cut a hardboard or strong card into a shape with two

DIAGRAM 71 (a) Hair styling: Plaits. Cut lengths of wool three times the required finished length. Stitch at the centre parting and centre back of the head. The fringe is made by sewing tufts of wool along A—B inserted under the top head piece. With matching wool stitch the curved front pieces over the tufts

DIAGRAM 71 (b) Bunches. Proceed as for plaits but do not plait hair — leave

it tied in loose bunches. This diagram also shows freckles

DIAGRAM 71 (c) Hair styles using plaits. (a) Plaits coiled at each side and stitched in the centre to secure. (b) Take the plaits to the top of the head and stitch in place. Cover the join with a ribbon bow. (c) Plaits folded across base of head back and stitched on either side. (d) Stitch wool to cover the head across the top centre down the back and neatly to each side of the head. Make a thick plait. Coil round to form a 'crown' circle. Stitch securely in place

DIAGRAM 70 (a) Hair styling: Alternative method of plaiting. (a) Mark the head into equal parts. Apply and stitch wool into each section. (b) Make a separate plait and stitch in place at C. This method is excellent for oriental dolls

DIAGRAM 70 (b) Hair styling: Ringlets. Twist several strands of wool together. Lay a finger across A—B, lift up at C. Still holding at C, tightly twisted, fold up to D on the head. Remove the finger and let the twisted wool twist onto itself. Stitch to the head under the hairline

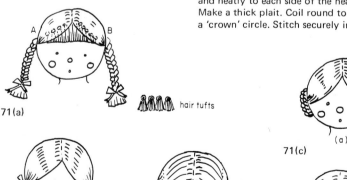

71(a)

hair tufts

71(b)

71(c)

(a)

(c)

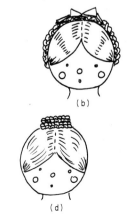

(b)

(d)

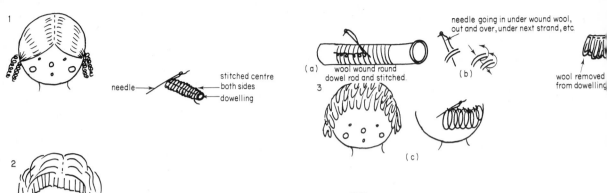

DIAGRAM 72 Hair styling. **1.** Wind strands of wool round a pencil or piece of dowelling. With thin sewing thread to match the wool stitch down both sides to hold into coiled shape. Stitch to either side of the head. **2.** Short hair style suitable for a boy or girl doll. Use thick wool unless for a small doll. Measure from side to side of the head. Stitch at the top centre parting. Stitch some underpieces round the hairline shape, and let the top layer fall on top of the sewn shape. **3 (a).** Make wool loops round two or three fingers or wind wool around a dowel rod. **3 (b)** and **3 (c).** Sew the loops together, then stitch in lines round the head until fully covered. Each line should be parallel to the first line with the loops hanging three-quarters of the way down the previous row. Strips of felt can also be formed into loops and sewn to the head as an alternative. **4.** Cut half of the top basic head shape twice in felt. Slit to make a fringe at the front of the head. Stitch it in place across the head, A—B

prongs. Wind wool round this template and stitch down the centre which has been placed on a strip of paper. Remove from the template, and stitch to the head, working in circles, applying by stitching down the previously stitched centre.

When applying hair to a doll's head never sew a top layer of hair to an underlayer. Each layer must be sewn to the actual fabric of the head.

Hair can be applied to a head by actually stitching the hair to the head as in embroidery, covering the entre head. Individual hair strands can be applied by threading a sewing needle with the yarn; stitch into the head piece, pull the yarn through until each end is of even length, then remove the needle and tie the two pieces together into a knot to hold. This method is very time-consuming, but as with other methods mentioned it may well have a use if making a specialised toy.

DIAGRAM 73 Hair styling. Pony tail. Method 1. **(a)** Stitch a bunch of strands together; lay them on top of the head, stitch to hold. **(b)** Stitch round the hairline. **(c)** Lift the front hair back over the face, and tie at the top of the head. Method 2. **(a)** A cord placed round the hairline and stitched to hold shaping is an excellent alternative. **(b)** Lay a stitched band of hair round the head where indicated on the diagram. **(c)** Lift the front hair over the back of the head. Gather all the hair from the back of the head and head base together and tie first with matching thread or an elastic band, then with a hair ribbon

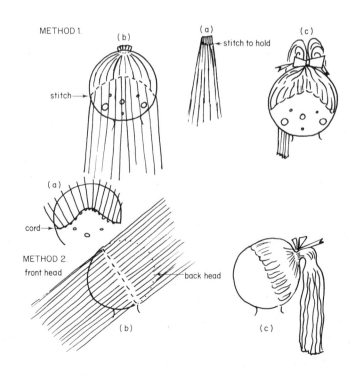

METHOD 1(a)

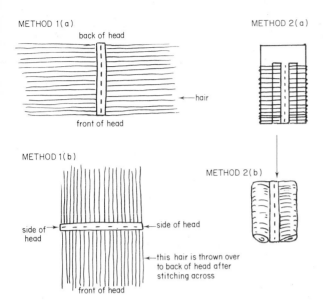

METHOD 2(a)

METHOD 3

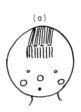

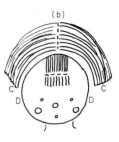

METHOD 1(b)

METHOD 2(b)

DIAGRAM 74 Applying hair. Method 1 **(a)**. Centre parting. Wool strands stitched on a sewing machine between paper or onto a tape. If placed between paper remove the top paper after application to the head. Method 1 **(b)**. Hair stitched across the head. Method 2. **(a)** Wool wound round a card template which has the centre piece removed. Wool is then stitched down the centre and slipped off the end of the template **(b)**. Stitch the curls round the head following the centre stitching line. Method 3. Fringe. **(a)** Fringe in place stitched and placed front to back of head. **(b)** Hair placed across the head from side to side. (Cut short, this method is suitable for boys' hair style.) Add length to the original measurement CC to give longer hair and it becomes suitable for plaiting. To hold in place stitch at D both sides of head and then plait the hair hanging free below this point

Applying hair into a slit

In the early nineteenth century wax dolls had their hair pushed into a slit at the top of the head and held in place with glued paper; the hair then fell over the entire head. This method can be used with a soft rag doll or with a model head. Wrap the hair round a piece of strong card or hardboard, the size of the card determined by the length of the hair. First measure from the top centre of the head to where the hair is required to end; this is the measurement of the width of the card. Wrap the hair round the card. Remove from the card and wrap the end of the hair around the top of the hair bunch and stitch to hold. This forms a tassel. Cut the looped ends. Place centrally on the top of the doll's head, spread it out evenly and press the knob at the end of the tassel inwards and stitch into place. If the hair used is a thick material and the knot impossible to hide, cut a small hole in the head material, neatly hem around this hole, then insert the top of the tassel into the head and stitch to hold. This method of applying hair is particulary suitable for boy dolls. If a curly effect is required this can be achieved by making a tassel comprising lengths of chain stitch crochet and applied in the same way.

Hair on a band

Wool or a similar medium can be machine stitched in loops onto a band of net, tape or gauze bandage, then wound round the head in a spiral and stitched to hold. The hair is then arranged into the style required. Always use tissue on the top surface when machining, this can be easily removed afterwards.

WHISKERS

Whiskers can be secured into the actual model during making up. For example, a lion may have an added nose piece, in which case the whiskers are knotted inside and then threaded out either side of nose. They can be applied by stitching through the nose from one side to the other, securing and threading back again, (see Method 1) or by securing with felt circles (see Method 2).

Whiskers can be made of various mediums. Black cotton or thread does tend to become limp in use, although it is soft if you want to use it in a bedtime toy. Horsehair is by far the most successful and very realistic. (Be sure to wash it in disinfectant and dry well.) For a firmer whisker on a toy which is more for show as a model, an old fashioned broom bristle is ideal, available from most hardware shops. Break the wooden broom

DIAGRAM 75 Hair styling. Short cut

measurement for hair length, and width of card

hair stitched or, if very thick, inserted at top of head

cut looped ends

hair bunch formed into a tassel and stitched at top

21(a). Wig cap. Applying strips of hair taken from an old adult wig

21(b). Wig cap stitched to shape and gathered round outside edge to fit onto the toy head. The wig is completely covered with the hair

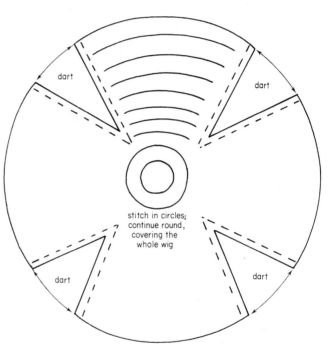

DIAGRAM 76 Wig construction cap. Used adult wigs. Excellent dolls' wigs can be constructed using a cap and applying the strips of hair to the cap stitching in circles. (See photographs)

dart

dart

stitch in circles; continue round, covering the whole wig

dart

dart

head to release the bristles, which are in small tufts with a curve in the centre. Individual pieces can be sewn into the toy by sewing at the curve of the bristle. Terylene or button thread can also be used. If making a character toy use the various coloured threads which are available — lurex for example. Whiskers do not necessarily have to be stiff, and droopy whiskers can look delightful on a mournful toy.

LEGS

Chickens, ducks, penguins, etc. require very firm support on legs and feet, unless they are in a sitting position with their bodies directly placed on top of the feet.

A standing bird with webbed feet can be supported by using two or three pieces of strong wire (depending on the weights to be carried), obtaining the correct measurement by measuring the length of the leg plus the length of the foot from front to back, adding an amount suf-

STAGE 1

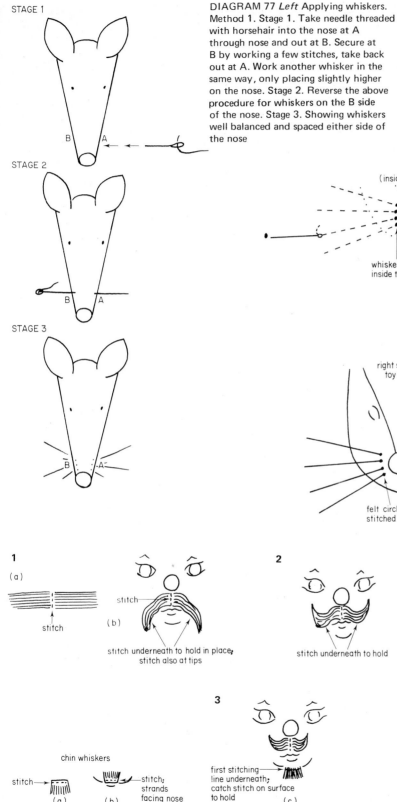

STAGE 2

STAGE 3

DIAGRAM 77 *Left* Applying whiskers. Method 1. Stage 1. Take needle threaded with horsehair into the nose at A through nose and out at B. Secure at B by working a few stitches, take back out at A. Work another whisker in the same way, only placing slightly higher on the nose. Stage 2. Reverse the above procedure for whiskers on the B side of the nose. Stage 3. Showing whiskers well balanced and spaced either side of the nose

DIAGRAM 78 *Below* Applying whiskers. Method 2. Another method of applying whiskers is to place a knot at the end of the whisker. Before the toy is stuffed bring the whisker from the inside to the outside of the toy in the position required. The knot will hold the whisker inside the toy. Cut small circles of felt to blend with the toy; thread a circle onto each whisker and push the circle until it is flush to the toy skin. Circles are either glued or stitched to hold in place

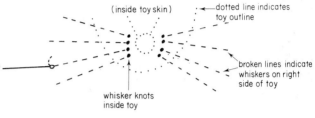

(inside toy skin) ←— dotted line indicates toy outline

broken lines indicate whiskers on right side of toy

whisker knots inside toy

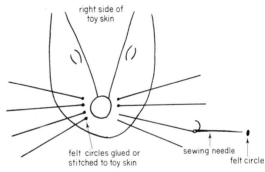

right side of toy skin

felt circles glued or stitched to toy skin

sewing needle

felt circle

1

(a)

stitch

stitch

(b)

stitch underneath to hold in place, stitch also at tips

2

stitch underneath to hold

DIAGRAM 79 *Left* Apply whiskers to a character doll. **1.** Drooping moustache. **(a)** Lay strands of whatever threads are being used and stitch across the centre of the strands. **(b)** Stitch the prepared strands to the face using matching sewing thread. **2.** Upward moustache. Cut the strands shorter than with the previous style. Stitch to the centre front of the top lip, underneath where indicated and at the tips. **3.** Short moustache and chin whiskers. Treat the moustache as in Styles 1 and 2, cutting to the required length. 3 **(a)**. Prepare chin whiskers by laying in strands and stitching across. 3 **(b)**. Lay the prepared strands, and stitch to the top of the chin with the strands facing towards the nose. 3 **(c)**. Pull the strands down over the stitching, and with small stitches catch in place on the chin point to hold

chin whiskers

stitch →

(a)

stitch; strands facing nose

(b)

3

first stitching line underneath; catch stitch on surface to hold

(c)

ficient to insert into the body. Bind these wire lengths firmly together with adhesive tape, holding the three pieces tightly together until the ankle is reached. The amount allowed for the length of the foot is spread out evenly to reach each 'toe' of the foot. Cut a piece of strong card, just smaller all round than the foot pattern piece, and use an all-purpose adhesive to glue each prong to the card. Cut two foot pieces in felt and glue one to the underside of the card base. Make a hole in the top piece to correspond with the leg placing and feed this over the bound leg piece. Stab stitch it to the bottom felt piece. Fold a piece of the same colour felt round the bound leg wires; stitch neatly. Make a duplicate leg and foot piece. Insert the top portion of the covered legs into the body of the bird where required, making sure the legs and feet are level. Stuff well within the body round the wire; only then is it possible to obtain a solid standing position. Inadequate stuffing at this stage will result in the legs appearing firm but in fact being very floppy in the body.

Birds — e.g. chickens — which do not have webbed feet make use of the same method, except that the leg is bound to the ankle as described and then each foot prong is bound separately using a strong thread or even wool, starting at each foot prong then continuing up the leg pieces.

Sometimes a fatter leg is required, and it can be very awkward wiring and then inserting stuffing into a small space. The way to cope with this problem is to bind the wire with the adhesive, then to wrap evenly round this with stuffing and in turn binding the stuffing firmly with thread. When the desired thickness is achieved cover it with felt as already described.

Curtain rings bound with yarn are a useful base for a small standing toy.

Twisted wool

If the legs are purely as a decoration, for example on a basic lying down outline bird, then wool can be successfully used. Either plait to form the legs and feet or take several thicknesses of wool and twist them together and let them double back on themselves, as for making ringlets for a rag doll. They are then stitched to the body. The toes are made separately in the same way, only using fewer strands of wool. They are then stitched to the main leg stem.

Rolled felt

Ducks' legs can be made by rolling up felt strips and stitching to secure. The base of the rolled leg piece is then sewn to the foot and the opposite end to the base of the body.

FEET

Feet for ducks and other web-footed animals are usually made of felt and it is sometimes sufficient to add pipe cleaners as stiffening. Birds can have their legs and feet made of wire and carefully bound with wool, or electrical tape covered by wool, depending on the size of the toy and strength of the wire.

When designing a toy the tendency is to be very careful with eyes, ears, hair, body etc., while the feet are the last feature to receive any attention. However, small details on feet can so improve the look of the finished toy. For example, an elephant has toenails; add these onto a finished toy and see the difference it makes.

Clowns look super with felt or leather shoes, open at the sole to display striped socks. Cats and kittens require pads added to their paws. Owls need feet rather larger in proportion to their bodies. Horses can have hooves added onto the basic shape of the leg and hoof by making the legs and hooves all in one piece and then adding an extra hoof front on as decoration.

Teddy bears can either have claws embroidered in embroidery cotton or, if a more elaborate toy is required, can have specially made felt claws. Ducks lying down need their feet stiffened with pipe cleaners and stab stitched.

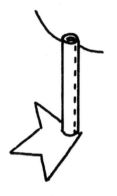

DIAGRAM 80 A leg of rolled felt, used for decoration only. Not strong enough for standing

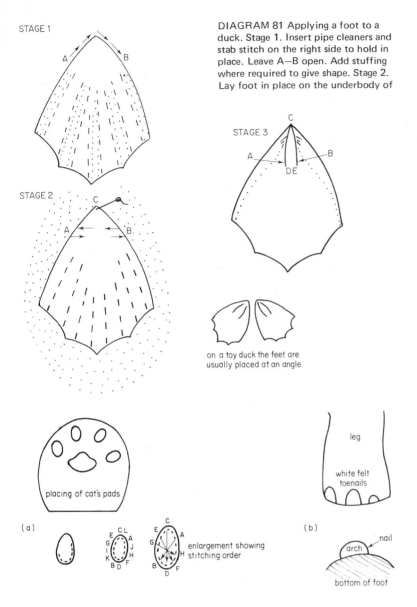

STAGE 1

A   B

STAGE 2

C

A   B

STAGE 3

C

A   B

D E

on a toy duck the feet are
usually placed at an angle

DIAGRAM 81 Applying a foot to a
duck. Stage 1. Insert pipe cleaners and
stab stitch on the right side to hold in
place. Leave A—B open. Add stuffing
where required to give shape. Stage 2.
Lay foot in place on the underbody of
the duck. Stitch from side A to side
B and then back again. Pull both sides
firmly together to make a ridge.
Continue upwards until C is reached.
Take the needle in at point C, pull
tightly and bring the needle out at
another spot somewhere on the
underbody and fasten off. Stage 3.
The result of Stage 2 will be to create
a ridge by pulling in B to E and A to
D. Do not pull the ridge too far down on
the foot. Keep the ridge contained to
the top of the foot where indicated on
the diagram otherwise it will cause
the foot to buckle

placing of cat's pads

(a)

E C L
G   A
K   J
B D F
H

E   C   A
G   H
B   D   F

enlargement showing
stitching order

(b)

leg

white felt
toenails

nail

arch

bottom of foot

DIAGRAM 82 (a) Adding felt pad
markings to a cat's paw. Do not stitch
round the pad full circle as this makes
sewing tedious and difficult because
the pad has so little working surface.
Stitch at angles A—B, C—D, E—F, G—H,
etc. This prevents the pad wrinkling and
is easier to do

DIAGRAM 82 (b) Adding toenails to
an elephant's foot. The toenails vary
in size. Apply the large nails first. Cut
the nail material — felt is suitable —
larger than required to allow 0.7 cm
(¼ in) turning. Ladder stitch the nail
to the foot; encourage the edge to turn
and become embedded in the foot
fabric. Form the felt material into an
arch as it is stitched. Fill each toe as
stitched with stuffing. Cut a felt oval
to fit the bottom of the toe arch.
Overstitch the edge neatly

Claws

Felt is the ideal medium for making claws or spines on, for example, a
dinasaur. Spines can be made, then stitched in place between the two body
pieces.

MANES

Manes are usually associated with horses, but on browsing through an
encyclopaedia you will notice many animals which have manes or tufts
of hair. This gives a very wide scope to the toymaker's ingenuity. The long
acrylic pile fur fabrics make ideal silky manes; felt is easy to cut into strips
and does not fray. Cut felt and fold it in half, then cut it so that it forms
loops. Lampshade tassels are ideal though rather expensive; wool tassels
are most attractive, especially if toned to complement the toy. Plaits look
pretty; suede and leather cut into strips looks expensive. Thick wool can
be sewn onto the toy in loops — the ideas are almost endless.

85

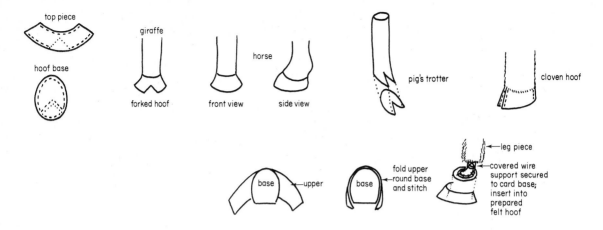

top piece

hoof base

giraffe

forked hoof

horse

front view   side view

pig's trotter

cloven hoof

base — upper

base

fold upper round base and stitch

leg piece

covered wire support secured to card base; insert into prepared felt hoof

DIAGRAM 83 Hooves   CONSTRUCTION OF A HOOF

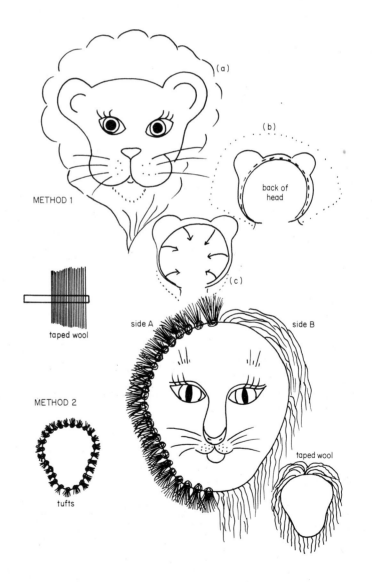

DIAGRAM 84 Lion's manes. Method 1.
(a) Shaggy acrylic fur fabric ladder
stitched round the face, behind the
ears. The point at the chin is obtained
by shaping the fur fabric. (b) Back of
the head showing wrong side of the fur
fabric and the stitching line. The dotted
line indicates the outside edge of the
fur fabric. (c) Back of the head. The
arrows indicate the fur fabric turned
to the right side over the stitching line.
It is then ladder stitched to the body
to hold shaping. Method 2. 4-ply wool,
four strands thick, knotted into tufts
round the face shape. (Side A.) Taped
wool — carpet wool is suitable — stitched
round the face shape. (Side B.)

(a)

(b)

back of head

METHOD 1

(c)

taped wool

METHOD 2

tufts

side A

side B

taped wool

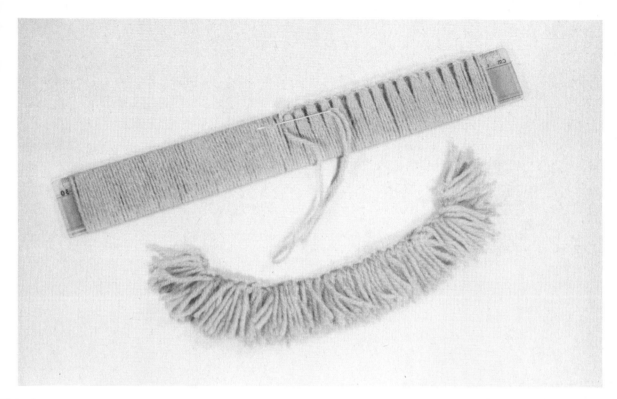

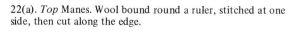

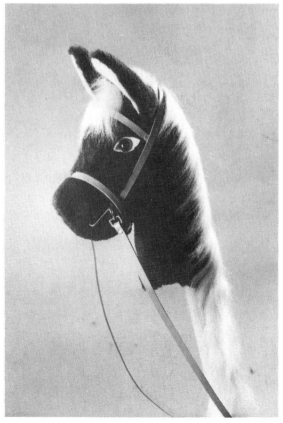

22(a). *Top* Manes. Wool bound round a ruler, stitched at one side, then cut along the edge.

22(b). *Above* and (c). *Right* Long acrylic fur fabric can either be incorporated into the toy skin or applied afterwards. The pile can be combed and parted into tufts, then folded over and secured with narrow ribbon bows

22(d). *Left* Wool applied to curtain rings with an overhand knot, then bound to form tassels. The rings are stitched to lampshade braid 22(e). *Right* Wool looped and bound securely to form tufts. Use a length of felt, fold in half and cut small holes on the folded edge at regular intervals. Insert a tuft into each hole and stitch to hold. The open ends of the felt strip are inserted between the two headpieces

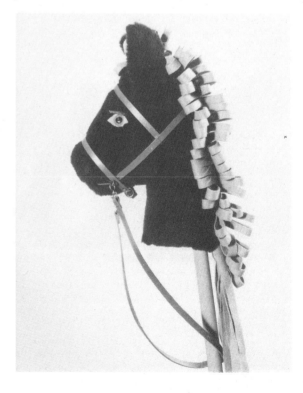

22(f). *Left* Lampshade fringing stitched to tape 22(g). *Right* Felt folded in half lengthways and cut into a fringe. Second layers can be used

TAILS

One very common problem encountered is when the tail is stitched, stuffed tightly, then attached into place on the toy body with the minimum of stitches. The result is a very stiff looking tail which appears to have no relationship with the body of the animal at all. Character can be added to a tail as with any other feature. Consideration to the wear it may receive is essential — for example, ears and tails are prime areas for a child to hold the toy by, so they must be attached very securely.

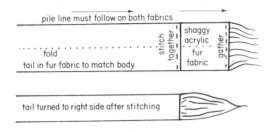

DIAGRAM 85 Adding a tuft to a tail

Firstly, some points about stitching and stuffing a tail. If the tail requires stuffing do so firmly but not too tightly. No division should be felt in the filling; it should flow in a continuous line whether curved or not, but it should be slightly flexible. If, for example, the subject being made is a lion with a tuft at the end of its tail, do make sure that, if the toy is made in fur fabric, the pile line of the tail fur and the pile line of the tuft follow one another. Imagine an arrow pointing from the top of the tail, where it is attached to the body, to the tail tip where the tuft finishes. If the pile lines match, the tuft will blend into the tail and not appear as an afterthought of the maker. Secondly, if you observe cats or other animals, they very seldom have completely straight tails. See the diagrams for ways of adding a curve to a tail.

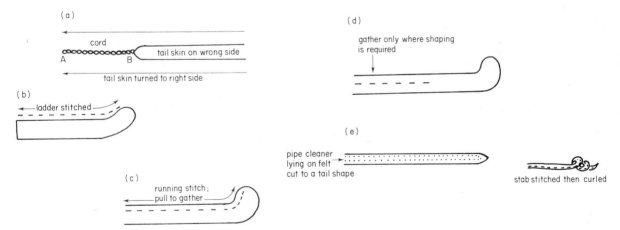

DIAGRAM 86 (a) Various methods for adding a curve to a tail. (a). The cord is cut shorter than the tail skin and attached to the tail tip B. The tail skin is then folded to the right side over the cord. Cord end A is attached to the body. Tail skin is then ladder stitched to the body. (b). The tail piece is stitched and turned to the right side, then folded in half and ladder stitched so that the tail skin forms its own filling. Pull on the stitching to form a curve.

(c). Running stitch to gather. For a full curve gather the whole length of the tail. (d). As for the previous method except that to produce a gentle curve — perhaps where necessary to add shaping without a full curve — only do a few gathering stitches. (e). Felt folded round a pipe cleaner and stab stitched round the outside edge. The tail is then curled as required.

23. Tails. *From left to right:* lengths of wool folded in half and bound securely at the end; lengths of cord folded in half through a plastic ring, bound at the end, then plaited and bound once to secure; felt tail, cut to a fringe, with 3.8 cm (1½ in) of the top of the tail, rolled at the top and stitched to secure

On a small animal, such as a mouse, the tail can be given an interesting curve by inserting a pipe cleaner. Pigs have curly tails, and a pipe cleaner is quite sufficient to produce a curl in the felt tail. It is inserted into the fabric tail, then twisted round a finger or a pencil to produce the degree of curl required.

NEEDLE MODELLING

To describe the technique as simply as possible, it consists of taking tiny stitches through the toy from one place to another, and pulling the thread tightly to produce dimples or recesses in the toy. Many toys are enhanced and given character by needle modelling. In its simplest form it can be used to make sockets for eyes, to shape hands and feet and add dimples to rag dolls. Needle modelling is also useful to add shaping to bodies of animals. A soft doll character may require padding and needle modelling to create the features. People may be rather hesitant about using needle modelling, imagining that it is a difficult process. Provided you use a strong thread and are prepared to give time to practising, you will soon develop the technique.

Stitches need to be as invisible as possible. Pulling on the thread to produce recesses also forms a contrast by creating fuller areas such as cheeks and chins. If you are creating a character toy and require wrinkles these can be created by using the above method.

Nylon stocking fabric can be used for covering dolls' faces and hands and is perfect for modelling a realistic toy. Thirty denier nylon is the best to use as it does not ladder easily during the needle modelling process. Nylon stockings or tights are manufactured in a variety of colours and shades and can be purchased at very little cost.

Needle modelling practice head

As with any process, trial and error is the way to really learn. With needle modelling it can be most useful to make yourself a blank doll's head, stuff it and secure the base of neck with stitches to hold. Now practise needle modelling and discover what you are capable of creating with a few stitches. It is inevitable that the threads used in needle modelling have to be secured to hold; this may well produce fastenings at the back of the head. This marking can be easily covered with the hair.

If the expression required does not come easily at first, try adding small pads of toy filling for cheeks, etc.

The nose may prove to be the most difficult area to needle model. To create a nose the thread is inserted in one side and taken out the other to form a ridge; if sufficient width is not allowed in the first instance the ridge will be narrow. Sometimes a face will become feminine in appearance when a male character may be required, or vice versa. For a male appearance square the chin and make a broad nose; femininity sometimes results from a too-pointed dainty chin and nose. When the needle modelling is complete view the head shape because pulling on the threads can spoil the back of the head. It may require additional padding or hair to return it to its original proportioning. If the needle modelled face requires a bald head, then add an extra back-of-head piece over the stitching and ladder stitch it to hold; additional stuffing can be added if required.

'Pouties'

An American term for dolls with a pouting expression. This expression which can look most attractive, especially on a baby face, and can be achieved with the careful application of fine stitches. First embroider a circle mouth keeping the diameter small in relation to the size of head; satin stitch would be suitable. With Sylko to match the skin colour of the doll surround the circle with six even stitches, pulling firmly to produce the pout. Bring the needle out at the centre of the circle, then take it back in again slightly away from the previous stitching hole. Pull tightly; this will make an indentation in the mouth. Fasten the thread. To add shaping to the mouth add a small stitch either side of the mouth.

Dimples

In cheeks, elbows, knees and chins. These are usually employed when making a rag doll in stockinette material. Always use the stockinette double or treble thickness, with the grain of the material running down the length of the toy. Without dimpling a stockinette-bodied toy can look very misshapen. To create dimpling always sew from one side of the limb to the other and pull up firmly. Chin dimples are made by taking the thread at an angle from the back of the head, bringing the needle through at the exact place where the dimple is required and then taking the needle back again almost through the same place.

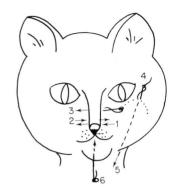

DIAGRAM 86 **(b)** Needle modelling a cat face. Nose shaping: **1**. In at top of nose. **2**. Parallel to first stitching. **3**. Working upards to forehead. Cheek shaping: **4**. Entering top of cheek. **5**. Bringing needle point out at neck. Chin shaping: **6**. Needle enters slightly behind protruding chin piece, out at point behind nose

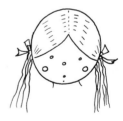

DIAGRAM 87 Dimples. **(a)** Front view: Dimpling at chin can also be used for cheeks. **(b)** Back view: The needle enters through the head at X on the dotted line, out at the dimple and then back to X again

(a)   front view

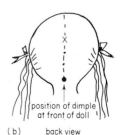

(b)   back view

8 Finishing a toy

ADDING ACCESSORIES

It adds considerable fun to a toy when it is not only dressed but also has accessories, a felt carrot for a fur fabric toy rabbit, a felt bone for a dog, a felt fish or mouse for a toy cat. A dressed daddy rabbit could have a waistcoat adorned with shiny buttons, and then a child's play watch removed from its strap, attached to a small piece of chain and inserted into a small pocket on the waistcoat becomes a fob watch. Tiny baskets either made or purchased containing felt flowers or fruit can be most attractive. Felt flowers can also look very pretty on dolls' hats and clothes. Turabast or raffia baskets are very easy to make by plaiting and then stitching and coiling the material — see the pattern for a straw hat and basket. By altering the shapes of the coiling one can create a picnic basket which can then contain a gingham cover and doll's house size plates, cups, etc. A small coiled basket without handles can become a pretty cradle for a baby animal.

A parasol or umbrella can look most attractive, especially on a display doll. Patterns are included for some of the above suggested items. Once the toymaker has become aware of the possibilities of accessories it will add a new dimension to their toy designs.

Felt vegetables, fruit and flowers

Making felt fruit, vegetables and flowers is a comparatively easy exercise, and they really do add attraction to soft toys. All that is required is either a picture of the item to be copied or a model.

Carrot
Materials
Small pieces of orange and green felt
Toy filling
Orange and green sewing threads
Instructions
Fold carrot in half A–B with the points C meeting. Overstitch edge C–B neatly and stuff firmly. Do not turn to the right side. Make sure the filling reaches into point B. Cut an oblong of green felt and cut the top edge into fringing. Roll up tightly and secure with a few small stitches. Gather round the top edge of the stuffed carrot C–C and fasten off. Stitch rolled base of carrot to greenery D to top of the gathered carrot top C. Add a few strands of orange cotton just above point B on the carrot for the

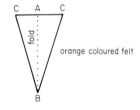

orange coloured felt

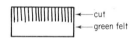

cut
green felt

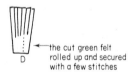

the cut green felt rolled up and secured with a few stitches

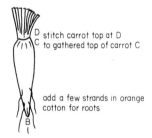

stitch carrot top at D to gathered top of carrot C

add a few strands in orange cotton for roots

DIAGRAM 88 Felt carrot, daisy and fish

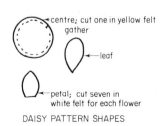

centre; cut one in yellow felt
gather

leaf

petal; cut seven in white felt for each flower

DAISY PATTERN SHAPES

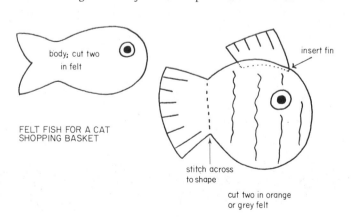

body; cut two in felt

FELT FISH FOR A CAT SHOPPING BASKET

insert fin

stitch across to shape

cut two in orange or grey felt

roots; secure well. Parsnips and turnips can be made in the same way making them in cream felt, with a darker green top and a slightly fatter shape at the top, C, and longer at point B.

Tomatoes and apples

Use circles of felt. Gather round and stuff; add greenery or leaves to the top. Fabric paints are useful for adding the blush to fruit.

Banana

Materials

Scraps of cream and yellow felt
Piece of brown felt for stalk
A brown felt-tipped pen

Instructions

Cut three pieces of pattern (a) in cream felt. Stab stitch together leaving one seam open where indicated to stuff. Stuff firmly and close the opening. Cut four pieces of pattern (b) in yellow felt. Stitch all pieces together where indicated half-way up. Add a few stitches at the top of each section and pull up to produce a curve. Insert the banana within the yellow skin and stitch the skin to the banana with stab stitching. Using the brown felt-tipped pen to mark brown lines down each ridge on the banana skin and draw lines as shading on the skin. The stalk is a small piece of brown felt rolled tightly and stitched to hold the roll in place. Stitch the stalk to the banana skin — see diagram 89 (c).

Doll's parasol

A rabbit or small dressed animal can look most attractive with an imitation parasol to match the dress. To make a parasol cut a circle of material and glue or sew lace or broderie anglaise trimming round the top edge on the right side of the fabric. Take a piece of thin but firm gardener's stake (or dowelling) and cut it to the length measured from the waist of the toy to the base. Cover this stick with ribbon by glueing it to the top, then roll it round the stick and stitch it at the bottom to secure. Make a hole in the centre of the material circle and put the covered stick through this for about 0.7cm (¼in), then sew the material to the ribbon on the stick. Gather the top of the circle just below the lace or trimming and secure it to the stick about 3.8cm (1½in) from the top. Tie a bow just below the top of the stick.

Hat and basket in raffia

Take three strands of the raffia each approximately 120cm (4ft) long. Stitch the ends together at one end only and attach to a door handle

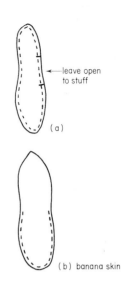

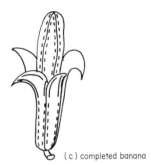

DIAGRAM 89 Felt banana. **(a)** Cut three pieces in cream coloured felt. **(b)** Banana skin. Cut four pieces in yellow felt

24. Coiling with raffia to form a hat and various basket shapes

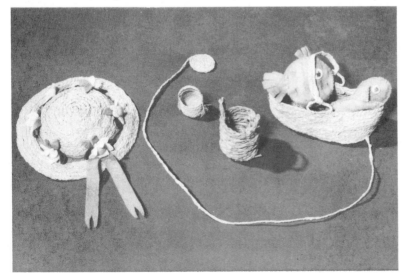

93

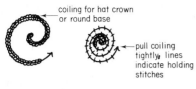

coiling for hat crown or round base

pull coiling tightly, lines indicate holding stitches

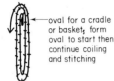

oval for a cradle or basket, form oval to start then continue coiling and stitching

DIAGRAM 90 Coiled plaited raffia articles

or hook. Plait firmly and neatly using the handle to brace against. When completely plaited stitch the ends together; it may be necessary to cut the ends level first. Start coiling the plaited strip. Form a small flat knob at one end and coil from this. As you coil, stitch the plait to the previous row; continue until a crown is formed of the required size. Start the next row slightly under the plaited circle to add depth to the hat crown. Continue until the required depth is reached, then form the brim by coming out sideways. When the brim size is reached fasten off the coil at the centre back of the brim edge. As more coiling is required whilst you work join the new plait by sewing the finishing and starting ends together, laying them parallel to one another for 2.5cm (1in). Trim the hat as required. A basket can be simply made by applying the same techniues.

DRESSING TOYS

Choosing suitable materials and trimming

It is essential when choosing material and trimmings for dolls' clothes to take into careful consideration the size of the doll or toy. Fabrics which are heavy or stiff will not look right on a small doll. The pattern size must also be a factor in the final choice of fabric. In some cases it may be wiser to choose a plain fabric if the patterned material available is too large for the subject. Cottons are excellent because they wash well and can be obtained in a very light weight. Woollens and velvets can be used for tailored garments, but they do not drape well on a small doll. Avoid materials which fray easily, such as rayon. Plain materials can be decorated with fabric crayons. Felt is an excellent material for doll's clothes due to the fact it does not fray, but of course it is not washable.

Designing a pattern for dolls' clothes

The tendency, unless you are a dressmaker, is to make the clothes too small. Even the smaller dolls can have deceptively rotund figures. It is wasteful to cut out the material and then find it is too small. Mens'-size strong paper tissue hankerchiefs are useful as they can easily be pinned to the dolls and being soft in texture they fit easily. Once the size has been solved the tissue can be laid onto card and a proper pattern made. By pressing soft tissues onto a doll figure you will get the finished size, but add on an allowance for seaming onto all the patterns.

Another method is to use the pattern of the doll and draw the clothes onto this, making sure sufficient width is added to compensate for the stuffing; however, this is using a flat silhouette while the doll will of course be three dimensional.

Having drawn out the basic pattern, simplify it. Consider the following questions. Does the bodice require shoulder seams, and can the top be cut out in one piece with a central back opening? If the garment is for a young child's toy is it wiser to avoid a fitting waist as this could make the removal of the garment more difficult. It is quite useful to dress a toy for a young child with the underclothes made as part of the toy skin and the rest of the clothes very simply designed to be removable.

Fastenings

Velcro (touch fastener) is a good fastening for dolls' clothes, especially for young children's toys. Sewing buttons on dolls' clothes for very young children is not advisable; snap fasteners are safer. If it is necessary to use buttons it can be time-consuming making the buttonholes. Buttonholes become worn with continual use, especially as the toymaker does not normally use the best quality materials for dolls' clothes. The solution is to apply snap fasteners and then sew the buttons on the front as decoration only. Always be aware of the safety factors; consider the material and its suitability to the recipient. For a young child the toy must have nothing in its construction which can be swallowed or cause any harm.

Trimmings

Once the plain basic clothes have been designed and made comes the fun of adding trimmings. Carefully consider the weight and thickness, and scale down the ideas so that the trimming is balanced to the material design. The whole effect will be much prettier if it is all to scale. Beads and buttons are useful, but only use them on dolls' clothes for the older child who is past the stage of putting items in their mouth.

As described under the section on colouring features, fabric paints are excellent for drawing a design on fabric. Another point to consider before adding trimmings to the dolls' clothes is whether the whole article has to be washable, and this also has a bearing on the use of colouring.

Braids add a pretty decoration. Lace is a delicate medium, and because it is so delicate it is less likely to look wrong. Broderie anglaise is very useful for making aprons. The strung broderie anglaise tiny flower trimming is versatile, and shows up particularly well on a plain, dark felt. Embroidery is possibly the most useful medium for trimming a tiny garment; however carefully trimmings are chosen they are still not scaled to the garment's requirements as embroidery can be.

Often all that is required to create an article which has instant appeal is the addition of suitable trimming; for example, a plain dress can have charm added with a white collar and a tiny narrow ribbon bow at the neck to blend with the dress, with possibly shoes and hair ribbon to match. Tiny buttons down the front bodice of a dress trimmed either side with rows of lace can look appealing.

A dressed male character toy, for example a rabbit or teddy bear, is much improved with a cravat and kerchief in a tiny pocket.

To enable the reader to design, make and trim clothes for their soft toys or models, diagrams have been provided to help with the choosing and designing of clothes' pattern shapes.

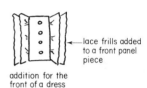

a white collar trimmed with a ribbon bow

lace frills added to a front panel piece

addition for the front of a dress

DIAGRAM 91 Trimming

Bodices

For the underclothes of toys choose fabrics which either tone with the top clothes or are in crisp white. It is good practice always to sketch the toy to be dressed and take note of the colour of the skin hair or fur and the eyes before deciding what colouring to use in the dress and underclothes materials. The finished effect will be well worth the consideration. Consult the diagrams.

1. Dress bodice which is also suitable for nightdresses and petticoats. Facings for button fastenings must be turned under along the line of the pattern.
2. Construction of a bodice.
(a) Cut a lining and tack in place — see broken lines.
(b) An easy way to insert a sleeve in a small garment is by stitching a continuous seam up the arm and down the side seam.
3. Bodice
This style can be laced or buttoned together at the front.
4. Blouse
Gather where indicated by the broken line. This blouse design is suitable for use with bodices.

Waistcoat, bolero, morning coat. See diagrams.

Dungarees, trousers and pantaloons

Dungarees

The dungarees have a lining for the bib incorporated in the original shape. An alternative way of finishing off trousers, shirts and dresses, etc. is to add a bias strip to finish off any openings or edges. On a neck band use a bias strip twice the width required. Sew with the right sides of the fabric facing to the neck edge, turn inside the stitch to hold.

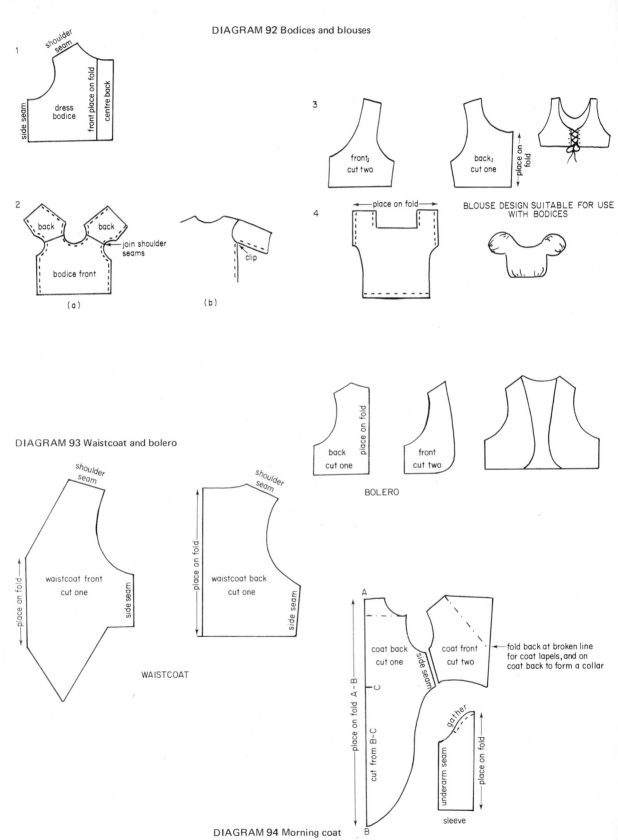

DIAGRAM 92 Bodices and blouses

1

shoulder seam

side seam

dress bodice

front place on fold

centre back

2

back

back

join shoulder seams

bodice front

(a)

clip

(b)

3

front; cut two

back; cut one

place on fold

4

place on fold

BLOUSE DESIGN SUITABLE FOR USE WITH BODICES

DIAGRAM 93 Waistcoat and bolero

shoulder seam

place on fold

waistcoat front cut one

side seam

WAISTCOAT

shoulder seam

place on fold

waistcoat back cut one

side seam

back cut one

place on fold

front cut two

BOLERO

A

coat back cut one

side seam

coat front cut two

fold back at broken line for coat lapels, and on coat back to form a collar

place on fold A – B

C

cut from B-C

B

underarm seam

gather

place on fold

sleeve

DIAGRAM 94 Morning coat

96

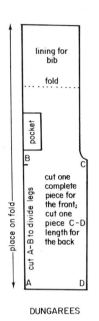

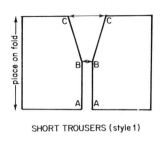

SHORT TROUSERS (style 1)

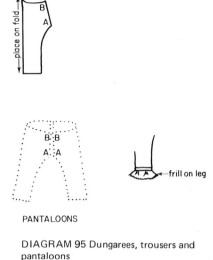

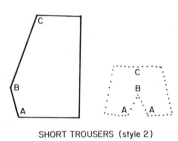

DUNGAREES

SHORT TROUSERS (style 2)

PANTALOONS

DIAGRAM 95 Dungarees, trousers and pantaloons

Short trousers (style 1)

Join A—B on separate halves. Join BC to BC for the front and back of the trousers.

Short trousers (style 2)

Join as for short trousers in style 1. This pattern is also suitable for making knickers.

Pantaloons

Join AB to AB. Add a frill to each leg end. Pin tucks around pantaloons and petticoats can look most attractive.

Aprons

Aprons can add to the character of a toy or doll. If a traditional peasant style is required, this can be achieved by adding bands of coloured embroidered trimming.

Short apron (style 1)

The shoulder straps are trimmed with broderie anglaise. The skirt material is gathered onto a band to fit round the toy's waist.

Slightly-shaped apron (style 2)

This apron is stitched, the secured at the neck edge with ties. The outside edge is trimmed with lace.

Half apron (style 3)

(a) Cut a straight length of material and gather the top edge.
(b) Lay a waistband onto the front of the apron on the top of the gathered edge. Stitch across the front attaching the waistband to the apron. Turn the band over the top edge of the apron. Turn in a hem and stitch at the back. Add a tie at each end of the waistband.

Long apron (style 4)

The skirt is just a longer version of the half apron. Bands of broderie anglaise are added for shoulder straps. The hems on the aprons can be done by hand or by using a sewing machine. Turn the bottom edge under as narrowly as possible, then turn under again to the full width of the required finished hem.

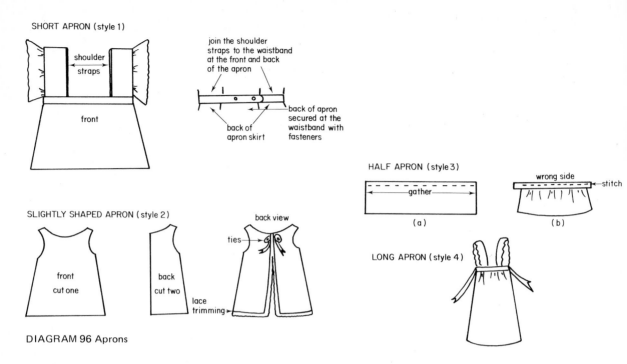

SHORT APRON (style 1)

shoulder
straps

front

join the shoulder
straps to the waistband
at the front and back
of the apron

back of apron
secured at the
waistband with
fasteners

back of
apron skirt

SLIGHTLY SHAPED APRON (style 2)

front
cut one

back
cut two

lace
trimming

back view

ties

HALF APRON (style 3)

gather

(a)

wrong side

stitch

(b)

LONG APRON (style 4)

DIAGRAM 96 Aprons

Nightdress

Gather the nightdress neck edge onto the joined yoke pieces. Further nightdress patterns can be designed by using the dress bodice shape and adding a gathered skirt. The sleeves can be made by using the sleeve patterns given.

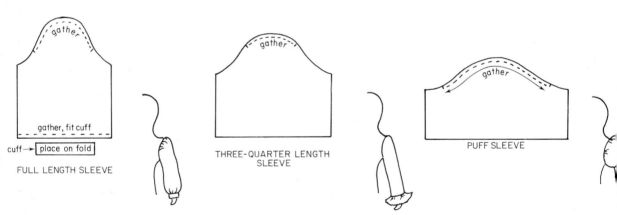

gather

gather, fit cuff

cuff → place on fold

FULL LENGTH SLEEVE

gather

THREE-QUARTER LENGTH
SLEEVE

gather

PUFF SLEEVE

DIAGRAM 97 Sleeves. Gathering on sleeves can be a single line either made by hand or on a sewing machine. If gathering a ruff for a clown character use two rows of gathering approximately 0.7 cm (¼ in) apart. Add a frill to a three-quarter-length sleeve to make it full length

Nightshirt and nightcap

Cut a strip of material. Join the seams at the centre front from A—B. Gather the next edge.

Jabot

This is an oblong of material trimmed with lace and buttons. It is applied to the front opening of the nightshirt where indicated, and sewn firmly, half jabot to half shirt front. The other half of the jabot with fastenings goes onto the second half of the nightshirt front. When adding frills always first hem the material edge to which the frill is to be applied. An approximate guide to measuring material for a frill is to allow two to three times the length of the edge to which the frill is to be attached.

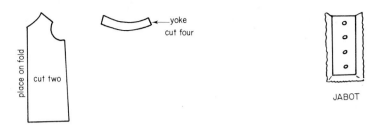

place on fold
cut two

yoke
cut four

JABOT

NIGHTSHIRT AND NIGHT CAP

DIAGRAM 98 Nightdress, nightshirt, nightcap and jabot

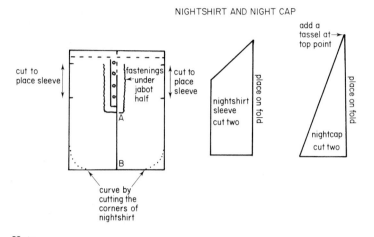

cut to place sleeve

fastenings under jabot half

cut to place sleeve

A

B

curve by cutting the corners of nightshirt

nightshirt sleeve cut two

place on fold

add a tassel at top point

nightcap cut two

place on fold

Hats

The method for making hats from Turabast or raffia has already been described.

Cap

(a) Cut five pattern pieces and stitch the sections together.
(b) The centre button is covered in felt to match the material of the cap. The peak is a circle cut in half with interfacing placed between. The peak is then stitched round the curved front edge and stitched to the cap.

Old-fashioned bonnet

(a) Gather the bonnet back where indicated.
(b) For the brim cut two pattern pieces in material and one in interfacing. Stitch the gathered back to the brim A–B–A. Add ribbon ties at A on both sides of the brim.

DIAGRAM 99 Cap, old fashioned bonnet and mob cap

CAP

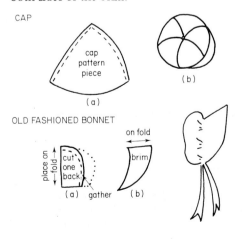

cap pattern piece

(a)

(b)

OLD FASHIONED BONNET

place on fold

cut one back

gather

(a)

on fold

brim

(b)

MOB CAP (style 1)

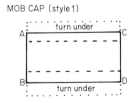

A turn under C

B turn under D

front view

back view

MOB CAP (style 2)

gather

finished mob cap

Mob cap (style 1)

Turn the top edge under on a length of material, gather and pull up tightly. Turn the bottom edge under and gather to fit the toy head. Fasten off. Join the ends A–B to C–D to form a tube using back stitch. If machining the cap, stitch it into a tube prior to gathering. Add bows for trimming as required.

Mob cap (style 2)

Cut a circle of material to the required size. Hem the outside edge. Gather where indicated to fit the head size.

Top hat and boater

See diagram.

DIAGRAM 100 Top hat and boater. The boater is made in the same way as the top hat, except that the brim and crown are circular

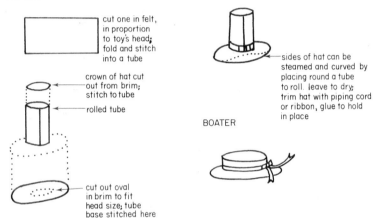

TOP HAT

cut one in felt, in proportion to toy's head; fold and stitch into a tube

crown of hat cut out from brim; stitch to tube

rolled tube

cut out oval in brim to fit head size; tube base stitched here

sides of hat can be steamed and curved by placing round a tube to roll. leave to dry; trim hat with piping cord or ribbon, glue to hold in place

BOATER

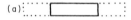

(a)

(b)

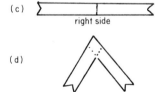

(c)

right side

(d)

(e)

DIAGRAM 101 Making a flat ribbon bow

A flat ribbon bow

This can be tricky with, for example, velvet, which is too thick to tie. The broken line in diagram 101 (a) indicates the ends of the ribbon, which are then folded behind and stitched together at the back. The solid lines indicate the finished size of the bow. Fold a piece of ribbon in half with the seam down the centre back.

Diagram 101 (b). Place across the bow and fold the broken line ends behind the stitch.

Diagram 101 (c). For bow tails cut a length of ribbon.

Diagram 101 (d). With the right side facing fold the outside corners down and fold the ribbon flat at the centre. Stitch to hold.

Diagram 101 (e). Place the bow on top of the fold on the tails and stitch into place.

Shoes

Suitable materials: felt, suede, chamois, leather (soft old gloves are excellent). Using non-fraying material with a firm texture will make the job of constructing the shoes much easier.

Laces are difficult to use on a small scale, but can be added artificially by stitching with embroidery thread. Buttons or snap fasteners, provided they are sewn onto the shoes securely, are suitable. Make sure the buttonholes are stitched well or they will stretch in use and the shoe will no longer stay on the toy.

The sole of the shoe, whatever the design of the finished article may be, must be of solid construction.

It is useful when making shoes for a toy to use the foot pattern, but it must be enlarged by at least 0.7cm (¼in) all round, depending on the material being used. Some materials, for example felt, will stretch on the foot, others of a firmer texture will not. It is also necessary to add addi-

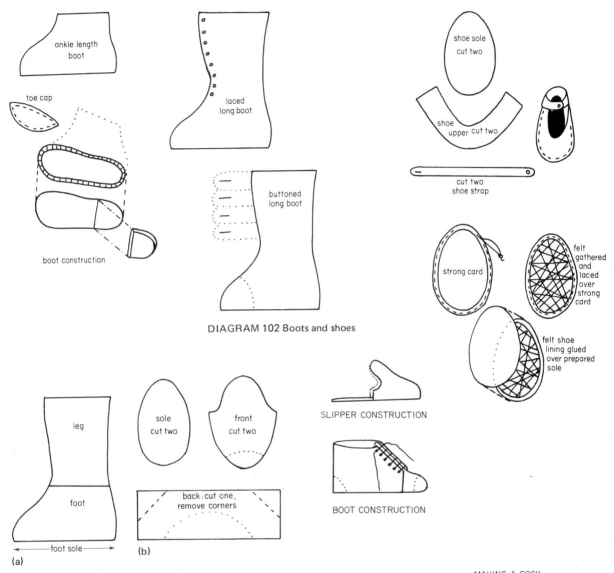

DIAGRAM 102 Boots and shoes

DIAGRAM 103 (a) Using a foot pattern to design shoes. Add 0.7 cm (¼ in) all round the sole piece. If wearing socks add further width in relation to the thickness of the sock material. Patterns must be enlarged to fit the larger sole measurements

DIAGRAM 103 (b) Boot and slipper pattern. The boot is constructed as for the slipper, adding a back piece and lacing

tional width and length to the shoe if the doll is to wear socks. The thickness of the socks must be taken into consideration if the shoes are to accommodate them comfortably.

Socks

These can be quite easily made using stockinette material, coarse lace or outgrown cotton socks. Wrap the material with the right side inside around the foot and leg of the toy. Tack round the outside edge, but not too close to the toy. Remove from the toy and backstitch along the tacking line. Fasten off, remove tacking and cut away any excess material.

MAKING A SOCK

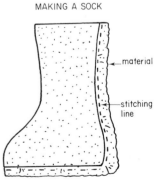

DIAGRAM 103 (c) Making a sock. Wrap material round the stuffed leg. Stitch round the leg shape. Remove and trim off the excess material. Turn to the right side

101

COSTUME DOLLS

These can provide an ever-continuing interest. There are many excellent illustrated books in the libraries both on regional and historical costume designs. It is essential to try and recreate the authentic costume details. When designing copies of the garments to create a special character it is essential to list the main points of the costume which are necessary to portray it accurately. For example, the line of the garment, the type of fabric, the sleeve design, suitable fastenings and the overall outline of a costume on the figure. Depending on whether a model or a toy is being made it is essential to consider various types of fabric which may suitably be used to produce the desired finished effect. If it is a model then it is essential to use genuine fabrics, not modern synthetic materials. Also, never combine synthetic materials with the genuine ones. Trimmings on a model should also be authentic. Quite often the older members of our community have bit bags with some very precious old pieces and are very willing to give these, especially if they share in the creating and making of the article. They can also be an excellent information source on styles of long ago.

FINISHING A TOY

When a toy is finished, do spare time to have a final look at it. Fur fabric becomes untidy with handling; teazle brushes can be obtained from craft shops. Brush the seams first, teasing out any fur caught in the seams, then brush the whole of the toy in the direction of the pile, seams included. Brush well where ears and limbs meet body. Make sure any whiskers are firmly attached.

Iron all the clothes of a rag doll well, as well as hair ribbons and trimmings. Leave the toy out for a while and see if you are fully satisfied with it — are there any additions you feel would add improvement? Perhaps extra features or an accessory.

The section on trimming clothes for toys can also be most useful for adding character to toys. Soft toys must be appealing and full of character. A basic shaped toy, can, with the aid of embroidery and trimmings such as braids, beads and sequins, become something special. If you are making and decorating a lizard type skin, then sequins can look most attractive. Sequins combined with embroidery are also most useful for eyes.

Care and attention at the final stage of the toymaking can bring considerable reward in the satisfaction felt at the appearance of the finished article.

Embroidery in toymaking

Embroidery stitching, however basic, can improve a plain toy and bring many compliments to the creator. For a small toy stranded embroidery threads are available in many lovely colours and can be used in various thicknesses up to six strands. A larger toy can look very effective when embroidered with thrums thin carpet wool, which is available in a wide range of colours, for example in blue/green and orange/lemon/brown tones. Choose a colour which complements the material it is being applied to. The main places to embroider are inside or behind ears, or backs and tails, and on paws.

Embroidery or fancy stitching can have other uses in toymaking; for example, on a duck or chicken made in felt, stitching in different lengths of wool in the same or a toning colour can give the appearance of feathers.

A snake can be given a forked tongue; with the addition of embroidery it can look particularly striking and be the main feature of the toy. Embroidery used in eye construction is described under the relevant section, and a suggested book giving a wide range of embroidery stitches is given in the end section.

REPAIRING TOYS

So often a toy becomes such a favourite with a child that it becomes loved to death; it is lain on in bed and takes part in many strenuous exercises, and the result can often be non-existent stuffing, missing eyes, torn ears and limbs and, if made from fur fabric, pile so worn that the toy is almost bald. The answer is not to make a new toy — which could never replace the old one — but, depending on the age of the child, to repair the toy. Firstly ascertain to what degree of repair work you can go. Will the child accept a completely refurbished toy or must the change in appearance be slight so as not to alter the toy's character?

Eyes

If safety-lock eyes have worn a hole in the skin it is more satisfactory to appliqué a felt composition eye. This will completely alter the look of the toy, so if it is not acceptable to the owner the only answer is to patch the toy skin firmly and then add safety-lock eyes.

Ears

Apply as described in the earlier section in this chapter.

Limbs

If they were previously stitched it is a simple matter to ladder stitch them back in place. If they were jointed with a joint set then firstly undo the seam nearest the joint and remove the broken disc halves, cotter pin and washers. Make sure the limb is firmly stuffed, then insert the new joint (see jointing section). Stuff the body firmly and ladder stitch the opening.

Head

If the head joint has broken open up a back or side seam on the head, remove the damaged joint and apply a new one, stuffing the head firmly.

If the head is not jointed but has developed a wobble all that is necessary is to open the body, preferably at a side seam, to stuff it firmly and then ladder stitch the opening. Likewise with the head, open a seam and stuff the head firmly, close the opening, then ladder stitch the head to the body. It is advisable to ladder stitch round the neck edge once, then to go round a second time with the ladder stitching slightly further out on the neck edge; whilst stitching round this second time it may be possible to push small amounts of toy filling between the top of the body at the neck and the bottom of the neck on the head; this provides an extra pad to brace stitches against and produces a firmly placed head.

The only way of combating baldness on fur fabric pile is to add clothes to the toy. In the case of a teddy bear an easy remedy is to cut out a simple shaped bolero in felt, attach two pieces of ribbon at each neck edge and tie them in a bow. A tiny pocket can be stab stitched in place, with a white piece of felt to simulate a handkerchief. Felt requires very little sewing, and is available in gay colours.

Repairing an old disc-jointed teddy bear

1. Either take a photograph or do some sketches of the bear in its original state so that you can retain the character and have a reference whilst you are working.
2. Undo the top of the arms, top of legs and neck edge to facilitate the removal of the worn or broken discs.
3. Remove the filling, and when replacing it in the body at a later stage make sure that it is the same as the original filling or comparable with it, as the finished bear must have the same feel as the original.
4. If an eye is missing match it as near as possible to the original eye, otherwise the expression will be impaired and altered.
5. Tint the nose and mouth, i.e. if the original stitched features are intact they may simply have become faded. If features are missing and you have no idea of the style of the original, study other bears of approximately the same age as the one being repaired.
6. New discs — often when you are stitching the top of the limb — show the original brighter edge of the fabric, especially if you have had to move

25(a). *Below* Repairing an old teddy bear. Bare torn pads, unstuffed body, one button eye and one original eye
25(b). *Opposite* Bear repaired. Eye to match the original one, new bow, repaired pads, re-stuffed, re-jointed and nose dyed. He also retains his original character.

the stitching line due to a weak edge. Trim the pile so that it matches the baldness of the rest of the bear.
7. Always match the thickness of sewing thread to the original.

CLEANING TOYS

Inevitably toys become soiled and it is not always an easy task to clean them. A toy made completely from washable materials and washable toy

filling presents no problems, although man-made joints (unless they are plastic) will not wash well. Dry cleaning is usually the answer but great care must be taken to expose the toy to fresh air to get rid of the chemical fumes. A quick dip in warm soapy water followed by a short spin in the dryer can be the answer if the toy is washable.

Some toy fillings (e.g. kapok), if placed in water and allowed to dry slowly discolour the skin of the toy. If the soiling is not too heavy sponge with warm soapy water, then dry naturally in the sun or an airing cupboard. Because of the bulk of the toy filling in, for instance, the main body of a toy, allow plenty of time for airing and drying; it can take a considerable while.

With some toys the filling is not washable, but the skin is. Undo a back seam carefully, remove the toy filling, wash the skin and, when fully dry, replace the filling and ladder stitch the body or limb together again. If in any doubt whether the toy contains filling which is washable or not, undo a seam and remove a small piece of filling. Usually it is quite easy to see if the filling is of an acrylic type, or kapok, foam chips, etc; if still in doubt test-wash a piece.

Never use very hot water; warm water prevents shrinkage.

After washing a fur fabric toy use a teazle brush and work all over the surface, fluffing out the pile. If necessary add a gay new ribbon bow.

Part II
Techniques related to specific toy types

9 Jack-in-the-box

It is thought the Jack-in-the-box originated in the thirteenth century. John of Shorne, a priest, was famous for his miraculous curing powers with skin diseases. One of John's miracles was to ask the devil to come to church and he would then confine him in his boot. As a result the villagers all made little boots with a toy Jack (devil) inside, and this is the possible origin of the present day Jack-in-the-box.

MATERIALS REQUIRED
Cardboard box or strong card; various coloured felts; trimming; a spring sufficiently flexible to be easily pushed into the box, but strong enough to press upwards and support the weight of the head and body constructions; either a round button and a scrap of thin cord to hold the lid down, or a piece of Velcro (touch fastener) for securing the lid to the box when closed; material suitable for the subject being made. (For example, the Jack-in-the-box illustrated was a rabbit, so it was made in fur fabric.); small tube section cut from the inner roll of a disposable kitchen towel; all-purpose adhesive; lightweight toy filling.

COVERING AND MAKING THE BOX

Covering a made box (method 1)
Obtain a box with a lid, with fairly deep sides. The one used for the Jack-in-the-box illustrated was 12.7cm (5in) x 15.3cm (6in) x 12.7cm (5in). To cover this box a piece of felt was required measuring 45.7cm (18in) x 43.7cm (17in); the additional 2.5cm (1in) indicated on the diagram by a dotted line was to enable the felt to be turned over the top edge and glued inside the box. The shaded areas on the diagram were cut and removed.

Glue underneath the box base first and place the box in the centre of the felt piece. Glue each end piece on the outside and inside the top edge of the box. Treat side pieces likewise. Using the diagram cut all the sides and the base in separate pieces of a dark felt, still with the additional 2.5cm (1in), as a lining for the box. Glue the lining into place; the extra 2.5cm (1in) protrudes, and is glued onto the inside edge of the base of box. Make sure you keep the lining level around the top edge of the box. Cut a piece of strong card to fit the base of the box and cover it with dark felt on one side only, allowing an extra 0.7cm (¼in) all round to turn under the card to glue it in place. This inner covered card will be used later to secure the spring. Cut a piece of card from the original lid to fit the top of the felt-covered box. Cover this with felt, one side in a light colour to match the outside of the box, one side in a dark colour to match the lining of the box. Lay this to one side.

Covering a card panel with felt (method 2)
Although there are many cardboard boxes available it is not always possible to find one of the size and type required. It may then be necessary to construct your box using strong card and again, as with the previous method, covering it with felt.

Using the diagram already given and the same measurements, cut out the base and sides of the box in separate pieces of card. For each piece of card you will require one piece of light-coloured felt for the outside of the box and one piece of dark-coloured felt for the lining. With this method it is necessary to allow an extra 0.7cm (¼in) all around each card piece because it is to be stab stitched all round the outside edge. Taking one

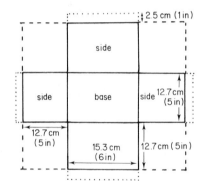

DIAGRAM 104 Covering a box (Method 1). Dotted lines indicate extra measurements on felt to allow for turning. Broken line indicates the corner sections of felt which are cut out and removed

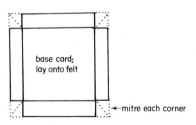

DIAGRAM 105 Covering a card panel with felt (Method 2). Mitre each corner for a neat fit. Cut first where diagonal broken lines indicate, then cut out the complete square at each corner

piece of dark- and one of light-coloured felt, stab stitch round the outside edge; fasten off. Trim the felt outside edge. Prepare each card piece in the same way. Construct the box by pinning the covered card sections together, then overstitch the sides and the base firmly together. The lid is then covered and laid to one side. Cut an extra piece of card to fit the inside of the base, and cover it with the dark-coloured felt as with the previous method.

Constructing a box by folding and glueing (method 3)

Using the diagram for method 3 score with a strong sharp knife where the broken lines indicate. To score you lay a ruler parallel to each broke line in turn; hold the ruler firmly with your left hand and with the sharp knife draw down the line, but do not apply too much pressure otherwise you will cut straight through the card. Apply sufficient pressure to break the top surface of the card only, and this will enable you to bend the card away from the broken line. Apply glue to one tab at a time and glue it to the inside of the box side nearest without a tab. Continue until the box is formed. To enable the glue to stick in the correct place it is a good idea to hold each corner tab in place with an ordinary clip-type clothes' peg. Remove pegs when the glue has dried. The box is then ready to cover with felt as previously described. The lid and inner base piece are constructed as per previous methods.

The construction of the Jack-in-the-box is the same for all boxes from this point onwards.

DIAGRAM 106 Constructing a box by folding and glueing (Method 3). It is necessary to cut one extra card piece to size of base for a lid when using this folding method

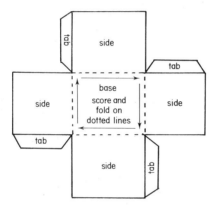

FITTING THE SPRING

Take the inner base piece of card which is covered with felt on one side only. Place the spring in an upright position in the centre of the card. The bottom coil of the spring is inserted about one turn under the inner base. Glue the spring into place. A few stitches can be added using strong thread to hold the spring securely to the card. If the card is very strong then stitching will not be possible, so add adhesive tape to hold. Cover the base of the spring to a depth of about 3.8cm (1½in) (on the size of the box given; adjust the depth in proportion to the box size you are using) with a cardboard tube cut from the inside of a kitchen disposable towel roll. Glue the base of the tube to the inner card lining base piece to hold it in place around the spring. Cover the outside of the tube with dark felt to match the lining felt. The placing of this tube guides the spring as the lid of the box is opened, and contains it as the lid is shut.

DRESSING THE SUBJECT

Body

If dressing a doll, clown or a similar subject, the body is simply a tube of material covering the spring. Depending on the size of the spring, measure material to make a tube, allow extra for all the seams and enough width to fit loosely over the spring. Place the wrong sides of the material together

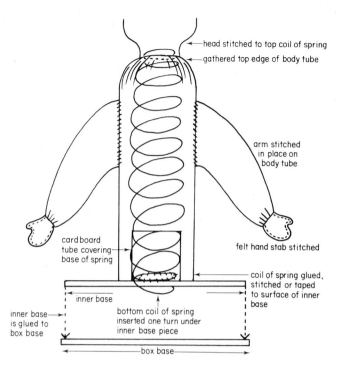

DIAGRAM 107 Construction of a
Jack-in-the-box

head stitched to top coil of spring

gathered top edge of body tube

arm stitched
in place on
body tube

cardboard
tube covering
base of spring

felt hand stab stitched

coil of spring glued,
stitched or taped
to surface of inner
base

inner base

inner base
is glued to
box base

bottom coil of spring
inserted one turn under
inner base piece

box base

and hold it into a tube shape; stitch down the centre seam. This will be
placed at the back of the spring. Turn up a narrow hem at the bottom of
the tube and glue to hold. Turn to the right side and place the tube over
the spring and the cardboard tube. Glue the lower hem of the material
tube to the base. Turn in the top edge of the material tube and gather
to fit the top of the spring. Fasten off.

Arms

Obviously the size of these will be determined by the size of the box and
the subject. Whatever the size of your subject all that is required is a
square of material for each arm, cut to the scale of your subject. Fold
each arm piece in half with the wrong sides facing and join two sides
together. Turn to the right side. Fold in a narrow hem at one end and
gather to form a wrist. Fasten off. Stuff lightly. Turn in the top edge,
press flat and oversew, making sure the side previously stitched will be
underneath the arm. Stitch to the side of the body tube. Prepare and
apply a duplicate arm. Cut out two felt hands and stab stitch round the
outside edge where indicated on the diagram. Stuff lightly. Close the
straight edge by overstitching. Insert a hand into the wrist of each arm
piece and stitch into place.

Head

According to your subject either design a suitable head or use a pattern
of a head you already have for a doll. Scale this to the size of your box
and spring. Make up according to the instructions. Use a lightweight toy
filling otherwise the head will be top heavy and will cause the spring to
fall over from the upright position.

If you are making a subject with long ears and you require the ears to
remain upright, glue a section cut from the inner cardboard roll of a disposable kitchen towel to the inner centre of the box lid. The depth of the
roll is determined by the length of the ears. Cover the tube with felt to
match the lining of the box and close the open end by glueing a circle of
strong card over it; this is also covered with a felt circle. The ears then

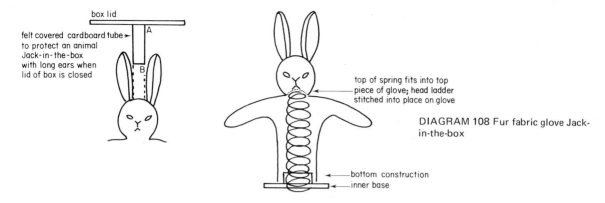

box lid

felt covered cardboard tube
to protect an animal
Jack-in-the-box
with long ears when
lid of box is closed

A

B

top of spring fits into top
piece of glove; head ladder
stitched into place on glove

DIAGRAM 108 Fur fabric glove Jack-
in-the-box

bottom construction
inner base

remain upright either side of the tube which pushes on the top of the head. This method requires a deeper box.

To secure the head to the spring it is essential to stitch the base of the head to the top coil of the spring. If you only stitch to the gathered material tube the head will fall to one side. Cover the joins by adding a collar or something similar to the subject.

Glue the inside base of the box and insert the inner base with the spring onto the box and glue into place.

An alternative method of covering the spring is to make a glove puppet body for an animal in fur fabric; lightly stuff the arms and the head and then insert the top of the glove into the animal head and ladder stitch into place. The glove is then placed over the spring and the bottom edge of the glove is glued to the inner base. Stitches are then taken through the neck edge of the head to secure to the spring.

INSERTING THE COVERED SPRING AND INNER BASE INTO THE BASE OF THE BOX

Method 1
If you covered a made box with felt then glue the inside of the box base and insert the covered spring and inner base onto this. Press firmly so that both surfaces adhere firmly.

Method 2
If the box was constructed by felt-covered card panels, the base can be left open at the construction stage of the box. The box base panel can then be glued to the spring base, and when all is completed the box base can be inserted into the box and stitched into place. Finally stitch the tip of a hand to each side of the box; this gives the impression of the toy climbing out of the box.

APPLYING THE LID

Method 1
Oversew one edge of the lid to one end of the box; this holds the lid in place.

Method 2
Cut two felt hinges; sew one end of each to the lid and the other end to the top edge of the covered box.

SECURING THE LID
This can be done in a variety of ways. Use two small squares of Velcro (touch-and-close fastener) and apply one by stitching it to the middle top edge of the front panel and the other half to the centre top of the front panel. Another way is to sew a button to the centre front panel of

the box, make a loop in strong thread or cord and stitch this to the centre front of the lid to hold it shut. It is advisable to measure your loop length carefully so that it easily reaches the button.

TRIMMING THE BOX

The trimming should complement the Jack-in-the-box toy which you have chosen. It should be colourful so as to attract the child or recipient, but the trimming should not detract from the subject inside or it could be an anti-climax when the lid is opened and the toy jumps up. The felt joins at the box edges and corners can be neatened by glueing or stitching cord or braid to cover them. Felt shapes can be glued in place. If a really elaborate box is required — for example, if you were covering the box in silk finish materials to go with a Japanese figure inside — you could machine appliqué shapes onto the material prior to making up the box. If your subject is a light colour (for example, a white rabbit) it will show to advantage coming from a dark felt lining. The reverse situation is applicable — a dark subject against a light lining. The trimmings will need adjusting also to stand out clearly on whatever background is being used. In the photograph of the Jack-in-the-box the trimmings simulated grass and flowers which were suitable for a rabbit to appear from.

10 Jack-in-the-box puppet

This toy character is constructed as an ordinary glove puppet. The lower edge of the body material is attached inside a box or cone in a similar way to the traditional Jack-in-the-box. A wooden spoon or stick is inserted right into the puppet, and attached securely within the head. The handle must extend beyond the bottom rim of the container when the puppet is extended to its fullest height. If a wooden spoon is used as the stick, the spoon part is inserted into the head and the firm stuffing of the head holds the spoon in place. This also enables the spoon handle to be turned from side to side to move the head in different directions. The movement of this puppet type is simple; the handle is pushed and the puppet pops out of the top of the container. Pull on the stick and the soft glove folds up and collapses, the puppet disappears into the container. The stick method replaces the spring used in a traditional Jack-in-the-box construction. It is best not to be too ornamental in the glove trimming as it requires to be soft and uncluttered to enable it to collapse easily. The head is the main part of the construction, and if the glove area does not fold completely there will be little room remaining to accommodate the head.

This puppet construction can be very useful as part of a puppet theatre production. For example, the container can be a nest with birds on a glove base as described; one or more sticks can be inserted and the birds pop out of the nest when required.

Several animal subjects are also suitable, such as a mother kangaroo as the main subject and an extra stick for a baby kangaroo to enable it to peep out of the mother's pouch. Try a cat and kittens with the container as a basket, or a cradle container with a baby stick puppet.

Make a rabbit puppet in your own style and construct a top hat in strong card covered in black felt. (See the section on dressing toys.) Attach the top crown of the hat to a hinge as described for the Jack-in-the-box.

DIAGRAM 109 Jack-in-the-box puppet; white rabbit in a hat. Diagram **(b)** shows toy withdrawn into the container after pulling on the handle end. If the toy subject has long ears they must be floppy to fit into the container. The broken line at X indicates the fold of the glove into which the top of the glove, i.e. the head and arms, collapse

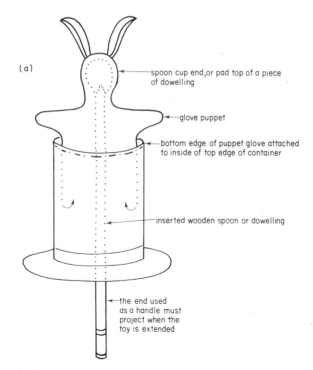

(a)

spoon cup end, or pad top of a piece of dowelling

glove puppet

bottom edge of puppet glove attached to inside of top edge of container

inserted wooden spoon or dowelling

the end used as a handle must project when the toy is extended

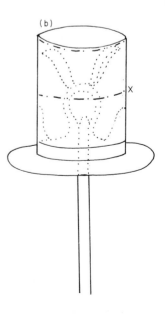

(b)

X

11 Knitted toys

Whilst intricate patterns can be very effectively designed for knitted toys, it is often the simple approach which produces the more appealing toy.

The main criterion is that the stitches are plain and of an even texture, so that the toy lining or filling does not show through the knitted toy skin. The choice of yarn colouring is most important; the toy should be as gay as possible. Knitted toys are a way of utilizing the odd balls of yarn left over from other projects, but do use yarn of comparable thickness in each toy.

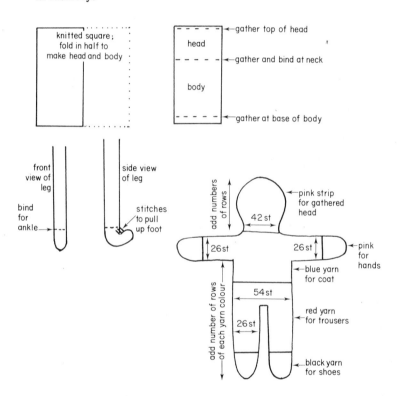

DIAGRAM 110 Knitted toys

A knitted doll can be constructed easily by means of knitted strips formed into tubes. To design a doll obtain or draw some squared paper. Decide on the height of the finished doll and mark this on the paper. Draw the outline of the doll keeping to a basic shape. Knit a small piece of the chosen yarn to gauge the tension and how many stitches are required. The squared paper will help you multiply the number of stitches per inch. Lay the knitted piece onto the diagram and you will see how many stitches are required. Mark the number of stitches onto the design. Double up the stitch total on pieces where you will be knitting both halves of the doll at the same time. The head and body can be one piece, stitched into a tube and gathered at top of the tube for the top of the head. Make

114

sure the join in the tube is at the back of the doll. The tube is firmly stuffed, then the base of tube body is gathered and closed. Gather round the neck with yarn and bind tightly to add neck support. Knit two pieces for the leg tubes, fold lengthways and stitch; the long seams should be at the back of the legs. Gather at one end and close to form the foot tip. Stuff firmly and stitch each top of the leg tubes to the body base. Bind at each ankle to create the feet. Add a few stitches to the top middle of the foot up to the ankle, pull to turn up the feet, and treat the other leg in the same way. Knit two tubes for arms and treat as for the legs; bind to form the wrists but do not stitch to turn up the hand. The doll is then ready to add features, hair and clothes.

When stuffing a knitted toy it sometimes becomes necessary to make a lining of material, especially if the tension of the knitting is inclined to be loose. The lining will stop the toy attaining peculiar dimensions at the stuffing stage.

If you want to design a toy for a young child with the clothes incorporated as part of the toy skin this can be achieved by marking on the toy outline at the graph stage each colour to be used and where colours are to be changed. It can sometimes improve the shaping and interest of a finished knitted doll if a knitted frill is added as a skirt, with the rest of the garment made as part of the toy skin, perhaps with the addition of a knitted bonnet. Braid can also look attractive as a trimming. Possibly add a felt or knitted belt where the trousers end on the toy skin and the coat or shirt top start. When applying features do not become too intricate. Keep them as simple as possible as this will look far more effective. 'Do not overdo a face, keep features to a minimum' applies equally to knitted and other soft toy designs.

12 Flat toys made from the stitch-around method

Draw the complete shape for the doll or animal.

Lay the template onto two layers of fabric and draw round the outside edge. Pin the material inside the outline to prevent it from slipping whilst machining or hand stitching. Leave a gap at the side of the body to stuff. If the toy is to be made in felt there is no right or wrong side to the fabric; however, courtelle fleece or similar material must be placed right sides facing prior to stitching. After stitching, cut the toy closely to the stitching line approximately 0.7cm (¼in) from the outline. If the toy is made in felt it can be left without turning; if made in another material, turn then stuff. Close the opening with ladder stitching or, for a felt toy, with stab stitching to match the stitched outline. If the toy is made in courtelle fleece or fur fabric it will be necessary to prick out the trapped pile from between the stitched seams.

Because this type of toy has no gussets or darts and the limbs don't move, they can be rather stiff in appearance, and it relies on the toymaker to produce depth to the toy at the stuffing stage. These toys are easy to make and are quite versatile. Additional interest can be added by using cotton material for the construction and fabric paints or crayons to add the features or clothes. It is advisable to keep these toy designs small; if too large they look clumsy. They can be successfully dressed or can be constructed with the clothes incorporated in the original design as part of the toy skin.

Animation can be added by stitched hinging.

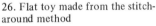

26. Flat toy made from the stitch-around method

13 Glove puppetry

The glove puppet has been a favourite since Elizabethan times with children and a source of great make-believe. Punch and Judy shows are still very popular today and in recent years there has been an increasing interest shown in glove puppetry by adults, possibly instigated by television.

MATERIALS

A glove puppet can be readily made from scraps found in a normal work bag. Felt, fur fabric and various other materials lend themselves to form interesting characters, but avoid materials which fray easily. It is necessary to select carefully the material that is going to be best suited to the character you wish to portray. Fur fabric is excellent as it makes a complete puppet that need not be dressed. Felt, if it is good quality, is very colourful and easy to construct. Furnishing fabrics also have their uses. Avoid using heavy fur fabric head and hands on a dainty lightweight material glove body — the material will soon show signs of wear as the fur fabric head will be too strong for it. Instead have a fur fabric or felt 'glove' and dress it. Another method is to line the 'glove' to give added strength. The reference to dressing puppets can be misleading as it is not necessary to have elaborate clothing. Any form of puppet, whether glove or string, often only requires the apparel to give the impression of clothes. Glove puppets are usually held nearer to the audience and so can be slightly more detailed, whereas string puppets are usually held at a distance, so any details of features and clothing have to be exaggerated.

INSPIRATIONAL SOURCES

Children's picture books are an excellent means whereby ideas can be obtained for puppet characters. It is also interesting how many ordinary toy patterns can be used to produce an animated glove puppet. The process is a simple one. Discard the body, leg and arm pieces, and use the head patterns only. Make a glove from those illustrated, cut to the approximate scale of the head. Make the head and partly stuff it, then insert the top point of the glove into the partly-stuffed head. Finish stuffing, but at the same time make sure the stuffing will not interfere with the movement within the top of the glove. Ladder stitch the head to the glove.

If a more detailed puppet is required add a tail or whatever extra features complete the character.

DESIGNING A GLOVE PUPPET

First choose one of the glove examples illustrated or use these designs as a starting point; you may wish to combine features from several glove types for your own puppet requirements. Think simply; avoid being too complicated for the first design. One of the most attactive glove puppets I have seen was a Chinaman, one plait down his back, two slit eyes and dressed in a simple oriental tunic.

Having decided on the glove style, draw or trace the outline.

Enlarge or reduce in size bearing in mind the size of the performer's hand. Make up the glove. Dress if necessary; the section on dressing toys may assist in the design.

Decide on the features; keep these to the minimum.

Consider accessories; a carrot for a rabbit, a baby for a mother toy, string of sausages for a butcher, etc.

DIAGRAM 111 (a) Glove puppets.
1. Puppet glove with tube neckpiece.
Hands can be added. 2. Glove suitable
for use with the three head piece
combination. Suitable for animal
subjects. 3. Glove with top piece to
insert into head. 4. Suitable glove which
can be adapted into a bird or a fairy
subject. Shows stuffed leg placing on
front of glove body. 5. Unstuffed legs
with stuffed feet. The top of the legs
have tubes inserted and secured to
enable the legs to be moved by the left
hand of the manipulator. The legs are
stitched inside the glove to the front
piece. 6. Ring secured inside back lower
edge of a puppet glove to enable it to
be hung inside the puppet booth when
not in use. 7. A puppet glove with arm
openings at the front for realistic
movement. 8. Sleeve pattern for glove
number 7

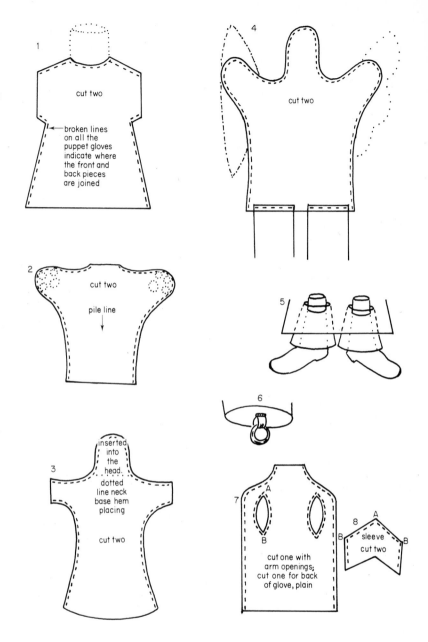

SOFT GLOVE PUPPET HEAD COMBINATIONS

Two felt head pieces sewn together
This style can be used with all glove types which have a neck piece to
insert. If using the glove type with a tube at the top of the glove, the
top of the tube must be covered to prevent the stuffing in the head falling
out into the glove.

DIAGRAM 111 (b) Glove puppet head
combinations

Two head pieces. Cut two head pieces.
Stitch together round the outside edge
leaving open across the neck base

Three head pieces

Two front pieces of the head are sewn together, turned to the right side and stuffed, then oversewn across the neck base. The third head piece is then added by sewing to the front of the previously stitched pair, then turned to the right side by taking over the stuffed head. The glove is then inserted into the head and the base of the neck of the head pieces sewn to the shoulder level of the glove. The puppet manipulator's fingers fit into the glove and up into the back unstuffed portion of the head.

Three head pieces

Four head pieces

Cut four felt head pieces. Cut two head pattern pieces in foam slightly smaller than the pattern. The foam should be approximately 1.3cm (½in) thick. Sew the head pieces together in pairs; turn each to the right side. Insert a piece of foam in each one and overstitch each across the neck base. Overstitch the two foam-lined head pieces together and turn inside out. The manipulator's fingers are inserted into a glove style, the point of which can be inserted between the back and front head pieces.

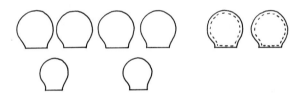

Four head pieces. Cut four head pieces. Stitch together in pairs as with two head pieces

Head combined into body shape

A very simple puppet can be made by drawing and cutting two complete body pieces combining the head shape. Cut one extra pattern piece of the head only. Sew all round the outside edge of the glove including the extra head piece. Turn the puppet to the right side and stuff between the extra head piece and one half of the body. Stitch across the bottom of this head piece joining it to one half of the body to keep the stuffing in place. The child's hand fits into the glove and up into the empty space between the stuffed front of the head and the back of the puppet. If a two piece puppet is required, cut two complete puppet shapes back and front without the extra lining piece. Do not stuff the head. The child's first two fingers fit into the head space. This glove puppet design can be made very quickly on a sewing machine in felt if a large number of puppets are required, for example for a school class. Supply the basic glove and then the children can design their own characters.

PLACING STUFFED LEGS ONTO A GLOVE PUPPET

Always place the top of the legs onto the bottom front edge of the glove. This leaves a clear channel for using the glove and leaves the leg movements completely free. If dressing the legs with trousers or pantaloons make sure the top of the legs are well hidden by a loose smock top or something similar which comes well down on the glove. The actual trouser legs can be tubes of material, stitched lengthways and gathered round the top edge, with the legs inserted and the trousers secured to the top of the legs.

GLOVE PUPPETS WITH UNSTUFFED MOVABLE LEGS

The legs are made as empty tubes, with the feet stuffed. A cardboard circle is cut to fit the manipulator's fingers and glued inside the top of

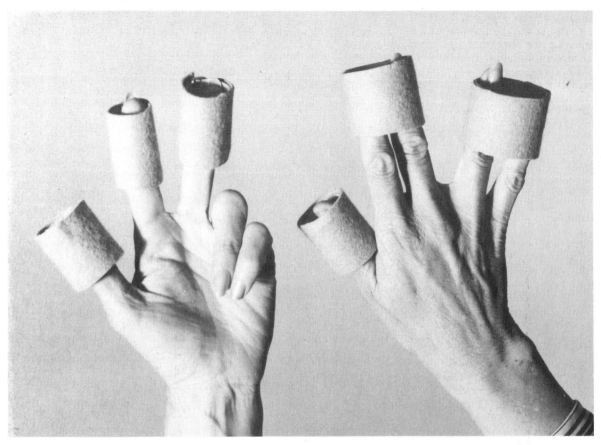

27. Glove puppet finger stalls to be inserted into a glove for arm/head/arm. The photo shows alternative finger placing

the leg tube. The top of leg is stitched inside the front of the glove and the legs are worked by the manipulator's left hand.

GLOVE PUPPETS WITH FOUR LEGS

To enable an animal to appear on four legs use an ordinary toy pattern, add a sleeve to the manipulator's arm and secure it to the toy. The back legs are stuffed. The manipulators thumb and third finger are placed in the front unstuffed legs and the first and second fingers into the head. There is no set rule as to the positioning of fingers into a glove puppet, however, and puppeteers can find the method most comfortable to them.

GLOVE PUPPETS OF A MORE INTRICATE AND DETAILED CONSTRUCTION

Moving on from the true soft toy glove puppet already described one encounters the exciting concept of glove puppets with ball heads, or heads carved from balsa wood, or made with papier mâché, etc. Here the earlier section in this book on processes related to soft toymaking will be most useful to the toymaker requiring a puppet of this type.

The soft glove can still be used although often a more detailed glove is necessary and the main difference will be in the head, hand and — possibly — leg construction. The same manipulation of hand movements may be used, but often the manipulator's second hand is involved when using unstuffed tube legs.

Various head constructions

A useful lightweight head can be made from a ball of stuffing covered with several layers of nylon stocking. The nose piece can be a small ball of stuffing inserted into the stocking which has been previously placed over the ball head. Thread can be wrapped round the small ball to create the nose. Ladies' nylon stockings or tights are available in a variety of colours, and are most useful if portraying a witch or a demon. The features and hair can be added using other sections in this book as reference. The head is then placed over a glove and secured to hold. A table tennis ball can have a hole cut in it into which a tube is inserted; the ball and tube can be completely covered with nylon or stockinette material and this forms the basis of a round head.

Papier mâché head
Turn to the earlier section on papier mâché. When constructing or moulding the head always insert a tube into the neck of the head to enable the head to be joined to the glove.

Hands
These can be made in felt, with wired fingers, or can be moulded in papier mâché over pipe-cleaner fingers. Insert a small tube or cardboard ring and stitch or glue to hold at the wrist. If the subject requires hand movement then you must have the means for the manipulator's fingers to control the hands.

POINTS TO CONSIDER REGARDING GLOVE PUPPETRY
1. The glove must be to the scale of the manipulator's hands. If it is too tight or too loose manipulation will be poor.
2. The main detail of a glove puppet is the head and shoulders. Keep features uncluttered.
3. If your audience is viewing from a distance, exaggerate the features.
4. Colouring is most important.
5. As with any toy, allow room for the performer's imagination and ingenuity.

PRACTICE AND STAGE MANAGEMENT
A mirror is most useful to practise any form of puppetry. It will show up faults either in design or manipulation very quickly, and these can then be rectified before a performance. A mirror will also help the performer to synchronize the puppet movements with the voice. In a classroom where one child may be working the glove puppet and another child the voice, it is essential they practise well to synchronize voice and movements; if they become separated the puppetry meaning, authority and authenticity will be completely lost.

A glove puppet stage can be as simple as a cloth laid over a pole placed between two chairs at home, or something more detailed for a public performance. A framework can be made by the handyman consisting of four corner posts with cross battens, the construction covered by material. The framework can be hinged for easy storage. The sophistication of lighting and curtains can be added, but make sure once you embark on this always to use qualified people to advise or do the work for you. Use a small shelf projecting from the opening of your booth for the stage; ensure it is at a comfortable height. Fix a lower shelf under the stage with hooks to facilitate the easy hanging and storage of the puppets when not in use. This lower shelf is also useful to rest the elbows on when performing the puppets. On each puppet glove at the inside centre back of the glove sew a ring for hanging.

A curtain can be hung across the inside top of the booth long enough to reach the manipulator's bent arms; this will hide the performer's face and shoulders while the glove puppets are performed in front of the curtain, on the stage. If several people are working together in the confined area of a booth it is essential that body movement is kept to a minimum and the whole performance planned to the smallest detail, moves included.

Scenery

Scenery can be used, but avoid it becoming too pronounced. It should be an accessory to the characters and as unobtrusive as possible.

Music

Movement of puppets can be synchronised to music rather than the spoken work; however, it is then essential for the movements to be perfect so that they adequately portray the story.

Group project

Glove puppetry is an excellent subject for a group project — there are many facets to the creation of a performance, so a number of people can be involved in writing the script, designing the puppets, constructing the performing area, and so on.

Part III
Adapting toys with a historical connection to soft toymaking

14 The Marotte

Originally the marotte comprised a carved stick with a head at one end with an ornate hat. They wore a deep collar which covered the musical unit which played when the stick was turned. In 1880 examples could be found not only with a squeak box but also with ivory sticks which were called whistle sticks. Marottes were sometimes called folly head dolls. Stock dolls were made in France and also in Germany, where they were known as 'Schwenkers'. The court jester in early times carried a short staff, and at one end there was a carved jester's head in the image of the jester himself. The jester sometimes called this wooden puppet a marotte or bauble. In some historical reference books there seems to be confusion between the definition of marotte and poupard, but the poupard was usually a more basic doll complete with legs and arms.

CONSTRUCTION

Make it in the same way as for a rag doll to the waist. A wooden handle or musical stick goes right through the doll and is attached firmly into the head. If using a solid head attach the stick into the head with plaster of Paris. The stuffed calico body goes to the waist, where it is tied to the handle. If a musical box is enclosed in the body it is applied in the same way as described for a teddy bear. The doll's shirt hides the musical element.

DIAGRAM 112 Construction of a stick doll

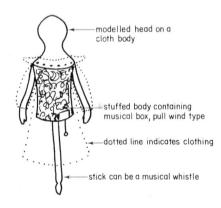

modelled head on a cloth body

stuffed body containing musical box, pull wind type

dotted line indicates clothing

stick can be a musical whistle

15 Two faced dolls

In 1881 Fritz Bertenstein made a bonneted doll which could be crying or smiling by turning a knob at the top of the head. This reversible technique can be applied to soft toymaking by the following methods.

1. DOLL WITH REVERSIBLE BODY

Add hair evenly to both sides of the head, so that a smiling expression can be applied to the front of the head and a crying expression on the reverse. A bonnet is used to cover the facial expression not being shown. The legs of the rag doll must be straight, with each foot a pointed or shaped end to the leg; by having no actual foot shape this enables the doll to be completely reversed. When dressing the doll all the fastenings of the clothes are on the doll's shoulders. The clothes design should be almost identical for both back and front view. Any alterations between front and back views can be achieved by the minimum of trimmings. Additional items, for example an apron or bolero, should be removable so that the child can reverse and apply them to the back or front of the toy.

METHOD 1

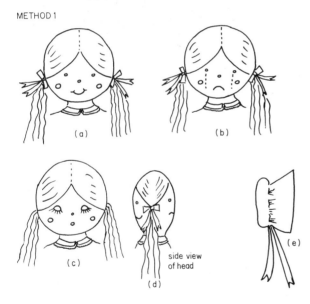

DIAGRAM 113 (a) Two-faced dolls. Doll with reversible body. Method 1. (a) Awake. Smiling. (b) Crying. (c) Asleep. (d) Ribbon must be placed centrally between the two expressions. (e) Suitable bonnet style to hide the expression not being shown.

2. KNOB INSERTED INTO THE TOP OF THE HEAD TO ENABLE REVERSING

The same principles of design can apply as already stated in method 1, although it is not necessary to have straight feet as the head turns. The neck of the rag doll is disc jointed. With this second method it is advisable to keep the size of the doll to between 20.4cm (8in) and 25.4cm (10in). Cut a piece of dowelling, the chosen diameter of the dowelling to be adjusted to the size of the doll being made. Use the diagram as a guide to the dowelling size in relation to the head size. Apply an all-purpose adhesive to the dowelling and bind the dowelling tightly with soft tape. Stitch the ends of the tape to hold it firmly and lay it aside to enable the adhesive to dry. Cut a small opening in the top centre of the previously stuffed head. Insert the bound dowelling well into the head stuffing, twisting it

DIAGRAM 113 **(b)** Knob inserted into top of head to enable reversing. Method 2. The neck is disc jointed. A knob is inserted into the top of the head to enable the head to be turned without removing the bonnet. The bonnet should be loose fitting to allow complete movement of the head. **(a)** Looped wool hair across the centre of the head. **(b)** Turning knob protruding from the top of the head through the bonnet. **(c)** Knob inserted into the head. **(d)** The dowelling is prepared by covering in tape which is glued and stitched, and inserted well into the head stuffing. It is essential to stitch the dowelling firmly to the head material

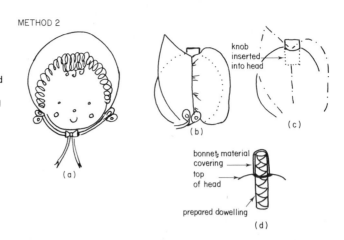

METHOD 2

knob inserted into head

(a)

(b)

(c)

bonnet; material covering

top of head

prepared dowelling

(d)

28. Two-faced doll body with a disc jointed neck and a knob on the top of the head to enable it to turn from one expression to another

from side to side to make a channel. Leave sufficient end protruding to enable it to be used as a turning knob. The dowelling must be well into the head. Turn a small hem and stitch around the top of the opening, then stitch the tape-covered dowelling to the hemmed opening; this inserting and stitching stage is very important, and must be carefully executed. Cover the protruding end of the dowelling with the same material as the bonnet, so that when the bonnet is in place the knob will be fairly unobtrusive. Apply hair across the centre of the head; the looped wool method would be suitable.

Apply the features, either crying and smiling or awake and asleep expressions. Make a bonnet; see the section on dressing dolls. (The design shown for technique 1 is particularly suitable.) An opening is made at the top centre of the bonnet to fit the diameter of the covered dowelling. Hem around the opening. The clearance on the opening around the dowelling knob must be sufficient to enable the knob to be easily turned to change the expressions without moving the bonnet. Whilst this technique enables a more spontaneous change of expressions, unless the doll is constructed in a strong calico and the covered dowelling well prepared and firmly inserted, then applied to the head with very firm stitching, it will quickly become loose and all the work of construction will have been wasted.

If a suitable piece of dowelling is not available and you do not mind the knob not matching the bonnet material, a very useful knob can be made by inserting a wooden clothes peg of the old type without a wire spring, and leaving the round top part exposed.

16 Double-ended dolls

The Doppelbaby of nineteenth century German origin has the modern counterpart in the Cinderella rags-to-riches double-ended doll. In Victorian times a popular interpretation of this type of double-ended toy construction was to have one half as a black doll character and the other a white doll. This type of dressed doll or animal is easy to make provided certain principles are observed, and they have a great deal of play value. The example illustrated is an awake/asleep rabbit.

CONSTRUCTION

Make two bodies and two heads. Lay the heads aside. Join the body pieces together round the waist leaving an opening at one side where indicated to turn the body to the right side. Stuff firmly; close the opening. The dress material bodices are applied over each end of the body and the bottom hems on each are turned under and stitched to the waist, meeting so that no gap appears through which the body would show. When choosing materials for this toy, choose two colours which complement each other, one for each end of the toy. Turn in the top hems of the skirts, gather to fit the waist and stitch to the body. The skirt lengths must be long enough to completely cover the heads. Check that both skirt lengths are identical. Turn up a hem on each skirt and tack (or baste) separately. Insert some trimming, for example lace or broderie anglaise, between the two skirt hems and stitch all together.

The arms are made as for a rag doll. They must be stitch-hinged to the shoulders for easy movement as they are required to swing either up or down whichever end of the toy is being used. When making the arms and sleeves it is essential that the sleeves do not impede the swing movement of the arms. Either make the actual arms in the dress materials prior to lap hinging, or hem the top of each dress material sleeve to fit loosely over the lap hinging. Ladder stitch the prepared heads, one to each end of the body piece. Add features and trim as the subject requires.

DIAGRAM 114 Double-ended rabbit

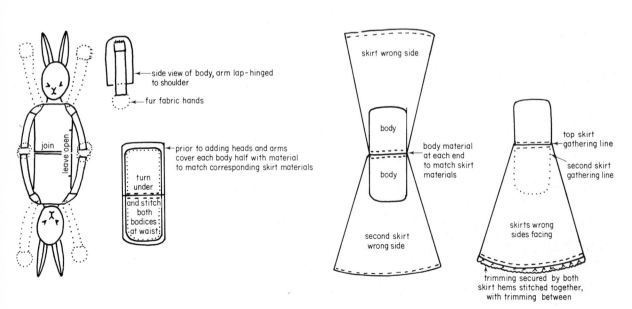

side view of body, arm lap-hinged to shoulder

fur fabric hands

join

leave open

prior to adding heads and arms cover each body half with material to match corresponding skirt materials

turn under

and stitch both bodices at waist

skirt wrong side

body

body

body material at each end to match skirt materials

second skirt wrong side

top skirt gathering line

second skirt gathering line

skirts wrong sides facing

trimming secured by both skirt hems stitched together, with trimming between

17 Pantin or Jumping Jack

Usually a pantin or jumping Jack is made in thin plywood with brass screws and nuts, cord with a wooden ball to manipulate the pantin, and the whole construction painted with non-toxic paint. It is usually designed as having seven separate parts, i.e. body, two arms, thighs and lower legs. However, as many as nine pieces can be used. Most traditional toys

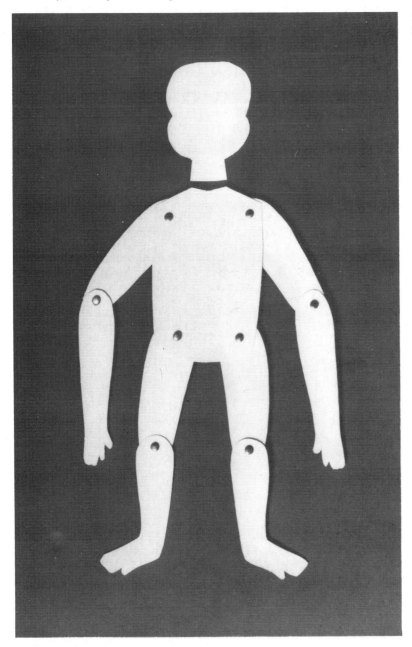

29(a). Pantin or jumping jack. Ten-piece pantin, front view

can be adapted into a soft toy form and the pantin is no exception. It can be made in strong card with the front covered in felt or fur fabric, or the whole card piece can be enclosed between two felt surfaces. The design must be completely balanced and symmetrical; design one half then turn the pattern to complete the second half accurately. When made in thin ply the shape is cut out with a fretsaw, then rubbed down and painted, with a final coat of clear varnish. When dried it is assembled as for the cardboard version in the photograph, but using brass screws instead of paper fasteners.

If using strong covered card pierce small holes at the top of the thighs and arms to which to attach the cord. Cut larger holes for the joints at the knees and top of the thighs and arms to attach the cord to. Cut larger holes for the joints at the knees, tops of the thighs and arms, lower than

29(b). Ten-piece pantin, back view

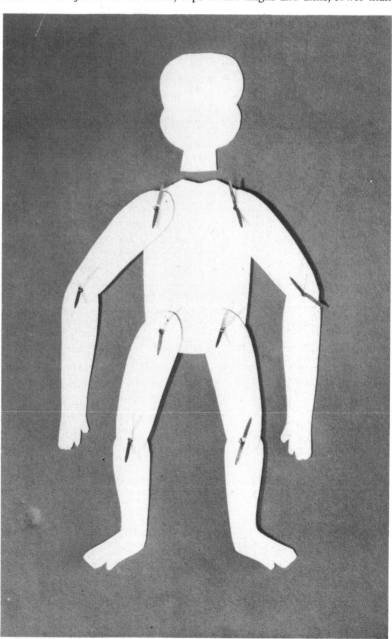

130

the cord holes. Press a paper fastener through the body where indicated and through the tops of the thighs; press open to secure. Likewise secure at knees and arms to the body at the shoulders. Do not pull the paper fasteners too tight otherwise they will impede movement. Tie the arms together at the top back with strong thread; repeat the process at the top of the legs. Tie these cross threads with a cord so that when the cord is pulled it will pull on the strong thread and the limbs will move. A wooden bead can be added to the end of the cord to give an easy grip for pulling. It will also add a decorative appearance and finish to the toy.

The monkey pantin illustrated was simplified in construction as the fur fabric would have restricted the movement of the extra jointing. If maximum joint movement is required in a fur fabric subject it is necessary to leave the movable joints free from the fur fabric.

29(c). Six-piece pantin, front view

29(d). Six-piece pantin, back view

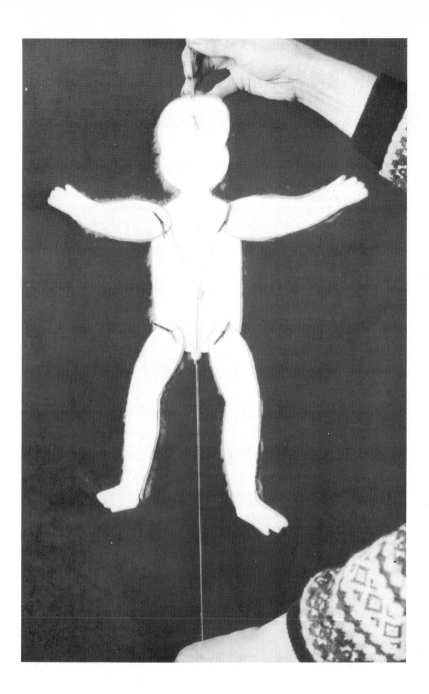

Part IV
Professional toymaking

18 Getting your toy designs published

People sometimes find that once they have designed one or two toys they gain such confidence that they produce really excellent designs; why not turn these toys into pocket money? Many of the women's magazines employ their own designers, but some buy their designs from anyone as long as they find them attractive. They do not pay large amounts for the copyright, and never use your name on the designs as more often than not they have their own house or magazine names; it can be disappointing to see your own designs with someone else's name, but it is still a nice feeling to see your toy in print — you know you designed it.

Firstly write to the Editor, asking if they buy original toy designs. If they do, make an appointment and take your wares to show them; very often they have a sister magazine who may be interested even if they are not themselves. It may not be your design which is wrong, but it has to fit in with the other contents of the magazine. They buy their requirements in months ahead so do not expect them to purchase one month and feature your design in the next month's issue. They will require the pattern full size, the toy made up for the photography if possible and full making instructions. Once money has exchanged hands it is no longer your design and you have sold away all right to it.

Some magazines have staff available who could help with the planning of the instructions. You pay your travelling expenses, so take all this, plus the cost of materials, into consideration when pricing your article. Never suggest a price; know how much it has all cost to produce, get to the magazine office and negotiate from then on. Make sure the model for photographing is well packed in a strong box; offices of magazines are notorious for having piles of samples of all kinds and I have seen my designs added to a pile of others in a corner of an office. A strong box helps a toy to retain its pristine condition for its photographic session. Editors usually get the photography part over with fairly quickly to avoid samples deteriorating.

If you sell a design make sure you are not infringing on any one else's copyright; you, not the people who buy your design, will be responsible if any problems occur.

Even if you have a well-designed attractive toy pattern to sell, you need to set out the making instructions in such a way that they are easily understood. Study the way well-known toy designers set out their instructions; never assume that the people who are going to make your toys know everything about toymaking. You are responsible for the standard of the toy they produce; they are also going to spend money on the materials and if your instructions are not clear their money will be wasted. Always carefully letter your pattern as this gives a basis to explain what you want the toymaker to do. Do a section at a time, e.g. body, head, ears, tail, etc. Never leave anything to chance.

Always do two copies of instructions and retain one for answering any queries from the magazine or public.

19 Making toys commercially

However well made toys are it is a sadly recognised fact that the public will go to craft shops and pay large amounts of money for a toy, yet it seems they expect toys made at home to be sold for very little. One must cost the price the article very carefully, as the majority of shops when pricing toys made by the toymaker at home add as much as 100% on to their shop selling price. If at all possible it is preferable to sell the toys privately rather than through the retail trade. So often the thought of selling the toys may tempt one to leave them at the shop as 'sale or return'. This is not advisable as the toys are continually handled, they soon lose their freshness, and the result may be returned toys that are no longer saleable. If several toymakers build up their stocks, then get together and have a market stall, this can be a selling outlet and the shared hiring fee could be very nominal. Carefully choose when to have a stall and adjust the content of the stock accordingly. Prior to Easter have inexpensive Easter-type toys, chicks, etc., if possible costing the majority of the items to under £1. At Christmas time the larger, more expensive toys are purchased, especially the large teddy bears and toys, often bought by people who are donating toys for raffles, etc. Control the number of samples which can be handled and pack the rest carefully in see-through bags.

In some towns specialized markets develop where local craftspeople get together to sell their work. Usually either a fee is charged for the hire of the stand or a percentage of the sales money is taken. Details of craft markets are often available at the local adult education institute or advertised in craft magazines. In some areas women's institutes hold markets where they are willing to sell goods, keeping a small percentage towards their running costs.

If the toymaker is, for example, a young mother making toys at home as a means of making pocket money whilst her children are small, then it may be a suitable approach to build up stock to invite people to a toy party and sell the toys this way. It is essential to price carefully below the selling price of comparable toys in the shops. Take into consideration the high overhead expenses which a shop will have which their selling price will reflect. Cost each item taking into consideration the cost of the materials and the time the items took to make. Try if possible to develop an individual style to the toys, or design an item which is completely original; this may then be the start of a cottage industry.

It is essential to keep an account of all materials purchased, time spent on each item and receipts for all sales, so that all income and expenses can be accurately accounted for, and when necessary declared to the tax authorities. It is a mistaken concept that the toymaker or homecraftsman will make a large income from their crafts. There are the exceptions, of course, where the items being sold are exceptional in some way, and it may develop into a really profitable exercise.

PRESENTATION
The actual standard of toymaking has already been dealt with in various sections of this book, but it is not only necessary to make the toys to a high standard because poor presentation may well loose possible sales. Set yourself a standard for your work and presentation. The toys will quickly take on the appearance of a jumble sale and become spoiled unless you guard against this in your display. Tables are supplied at craft markets and similar venues, but if you are selling in a private house you may have unsuitable tables that are too wide or too small; you may only be allocated

a corner of a table. If your selling parties seem to be successful it may well be more professional to purchase a folding wallpaper pasting table. These are inexpensive, have a carrying handle, are lightweight and fit easily into a car. Either make a fitted cover for the table measuring to ground level at the front and ends or use a cloth to cover it. Felt, hessian or cotton materials are all suitable. A dark colour — blue or brown — will act as a contrast to the brighter toy fabrics. Cover a variety of cardboard boxes in different sizes with fabric matching the table drapes; these will give height to your display and also show individual toy items in a clear, uncluttered manner. Spare toys can be stored in boxes under the table; as the table cover is to floor level the stored items will be neatly out of sight. Clearly price each item using either stick-on price labels or the type with a cotton loop for threading a tag onto a toy's ribbon, bow, etc. These can also be tied onto elastic bands, and the band attached to a toy arm or leg. Never use ordinary pins for attaching a price tag to a toy.

If selling a variety of toy subjects try and have available a range of colour choices but have an order book with you so that you can offer to make the toy for the customer in some other colour. Use a duplicate book, write out the order, give the customer the top portion and retain the duplicate in your book. It is preferable to take a small deposit of money on the order and this should be clearly shown on the invoice. A customer is more likely to remember and honour a transaction which they have already subscribed to. Plan your orders carefully, taking into consideration the date the client may require the toy by, and balance your orders against the time you have available to make them. If you overbook your time the result could well be a lowering of your toymaking standards and subsequently fewer sales.

It is a good policy to give your business a name; customers are more likely to remember your toys then. This is particularly necessary at functions where you may be in competition with other toymakers. A good means of advertisement is to have printed cards with your name, address and telephone number to hand out to interested customers who may give you orders at a future date.

20 Showing and exhibiting toys

It is essential to remember the following points:
1. Read the show schedule carefully, and conform exactly to its requirements. It is surprising the large numbers of exhibits which have to be regretfully disqualified because they vary in content from the schedule.
2. Note the times of arrival, allocation of space and the time permitted for exhibition prior to judging. Carefully complete the entry form and send it off in plenty of time prior to the closing date. Make sure you are aware of the times the show is open to the public and the stated time for removing the exhibits after the show.

POINTS JUDGES TAKE INTO CONSIDERATION

Fur fabric toys
(a) Direction of fur-pile line and how it is presented, i.e. if well brushed with no pile caught between the seams.
(b) Whether the seams show due to bad cutting out and stitching.
(c) Positioning of eyes.
(d) Paws, pads and noses must be well sewn to the toy without any ridges in material.
(e) Expression.
(f) Whether tails and ears look part of the toy or if they appear sewn on as an afterthought.
(g) Colour choice.
(h) Stuffing; most important. Examined to see if the stuffing really moulds the toy and reaches all corners of the toy skin. It should be smooth with no unsightly bumps.
(i) Character and play value; whether the choice of subject is suitable for the schedule requirements.
(j) If the toy is wired no part of the wiring should be felt through the toy skin.
(k) Legs on a standing toy should be well balanced and firm.
(l) A jointed toy must have tight joints. No neck wobble. Legs must be level at base.
(m) All felt features should be stitched firmly in place.
(n) Whiskers must not be able to be pulled out.

Rag dolls
(a) Stitching of body should be neat and smooth with careful attention to hands.
(b) Unless the doll is designed as a floppy character, it should have firm neck support.
(c) Colouring and general appeal of the features. The application of features, whether neatly applied or easily plucked off by young fingers. Choice of the skin tone.
(d) Application, design and balance of hair in relation to the toy character being portrayed.
(e) Dress appeal. Whether easily removed by small hands. How well the fastenings and trimmings are sewn to cope with excessive wear. Whether all items are washable on a doll which is intended to be fully washable.
(f) Stuffing. The face front should be very smooth to set off the features. The stuffing should reach all the extremities. Use of the correct toy filling colour to retain the clear tone of the toy skin.
(g) General finishing off, i.e. trimmings on garments, ribbon on hair, whether shoes fit the doll well. Special attention to the soles on the shoes.

137

(h) Originality of design, and in some cases marks are added for suitable accessories, if permitted in schedule description. Design suitability in relation to recipient's age and, most important, the play value.

Patchwork toys
(a) Material weights, whether comparable.
(b) Fabric types should not be mixed.
(c) Threads. In the past only black or white threads were used for joining the patches; now coloured threads are permissible. Threads should be of a fine texture.
(d) Stitches should be small and even.
(e) The joining of patches must be carefully executed, especially at corners and points.
(f) Design related to colouring.
(g) Suitable use of the patchwork shapes in relation to the toy; also colour tones.

Knitted toys
(a) Tension must be even.
(b) Stuffing should be lightweight and not show through the toy skin.
(c) Features should lay smoothly and not be pulled tightly to distort the toy skin.
(d) Seams should be flat.
(e) Design, colouring, suitability of subject.

It is impossible in the space allocated to cover the aspects of all toys; the general points discussed under each section are relevant to many toy types, particularly colouring, design and the finish of the toy. Safety factors must always be carefully considered. All the sections under the techniques in this book show how a toy should be made; therefore these automatically cover the points related to judging or exhibiting.

JUDGING
If the techniques described in this book are put into practice you may well be asked to judge at a show. The techniques you will already know; however, a few words on etiquette and proceedings. You should be formally invited to judge by letter. Carefully check and book the date if convenient to you. Ensure in your letter of acceptance that you clearly state any fees you require. If the show organizers are efficient you should receive the schedule ahead of the show date. Carefully read not only your relevant section but also the general show rules. Note the time of judging and the system of awards, check whether there are any special cups to be awarded in your section. On the show day allow plenty of travelling time; arrive at least a half an hour before judging commences. This will enable the actual location of the exhibits, etc. to be found. Report to the show secretary on arrival.

Items to have with you for judging
Clipboard, schedule, judge's comment slips, apron, pen or pencil. (When making comments on the article never write with felt-tipped pen near any article; this could result in soiling.) Pins for attaching comment slip to exhibitor's card (not to toy).

Comment slips
When making comments they must be constructive, otherwise you may dissuade the exhibitor from ever entering a competitive show again. Try and find a good point to praise the toymaker for, then add any criticism. Judging should be a teaching situation with the judge, giving the exhibitor the benefit of their knowledge. It should also be a two-way process, with the judge at all times learning from the exhibitor's prowess. The judge should never inflict opinion, rather than knowledge, onto the exhibitor. To be a good judge all personal preferences for colour, design, etc. should

be ignored; instead, the judge should view the toy, if possible, through the exhibitor's eyes. They should weigh up in their minds why the exhibitor chose a particular colour or style and look for all these facts before making a final assessment of the work. It can be so easy to fall into the trap of liking a particular toy because it fits your concepts; it is much harder to choose a toy which has all the attributes of being well made, but in a form which is alien to your individual choice and style.

Never be tempted to return to the show when it is open to the public; if you hear criticisms or questions related to your judging you will be tempted to reply. Rest on the fact that the judges decision is final! Do not judge at venues too near your home; even though you do not see the exhibitors' names, you may recognise an article, or in all innocence give the award to a toy which you then discover was made by a friend or acquaintance. If it is discovered you were the judge, doubts on your impartiality can quickly develop.

Bibliography

Baroness de Sanguiy, *Good Design in Soft Toys,* Mills & Boon, 1971.
Cockett, Mary, *Dolls and Puppets,* David & Charles, Newton Abbot, 1974.
Dyer, Anne, *Design Your Own Stuffed Toys,* Bell, 1969.
Hillier, Mary, *Dolls and Dollmakers,* Weidenfeld & Nicolson, 1968.
Hutchings, Margaret, *Dolls and How to Make Them*, Mills & Boon, 1980.
Hutchings, Margaret, *Teddy Bears and How to Make Them*, Mills & Boon, 1964, reprinted, Dover Publications, 1977.
Peake, Pamela, *The Complete Book of Soft Dolls*, David & Charles, Newton Abbot, 1979.
Snook, Barbara, *Embroidery Stitches*, Batsford, 1981.

List of craft suppliers

U.K.

All toymaking materials are available from Granary Crafts, Bookham, Surrey.

Fur fabrics, toy fillings, toy patterns.
Beckfoot Mills,
Beckfoot Lane,
Harden,
Bingley,
West Yorkshire,
BD16 1AR.

Toy joints, bells, squeakers, chimes, growlers.

Margrave Manufacturing Co Ltd.,
Margrave Works,
London,
SW6 4TJ.

Toy eyes.

Lynne Oliver Toy Components Ltd.,
2 New Steien Mews,
St James's Street,
Brighton,
Sussex,
BN2 1QP.

Fur fabrics, toy fillings, components, eyes, noses (etc.), bells.

Homecraft Supplies Ltd.,
27 Trinity Road,
London,
SW17.

Fur fabrics, toy fillings.

Fluffy Fabrics,
Unit N1/N2 Tribune Drive,
Trinity Trading Estate,
Sittingbourne,
Kent.

Trimmings, buckles, feathers, materials.

John Lewis,
Oxford Street,
London W1.

Dolls, wigs.

Mail Order Dept.,
The Handicraft Shop,
47 Northgate,
Canterbury,
Kent,
CT1 1BE.

Catalogues are available from the above firms but it is advisable to send postage.

Musical movements (all types).

W. Hobby Ltd.,
Knight's Hill Square,
London,
SE27 0HH.

Polyfilla (a type of plaster);
Polycell (a wallpaper adhesive).

Available from home decorating stockists.

Gesso Powder (a finely ground powder which is mixed with water to a creamy consistency, drying relatively hard with adhesive to the surface to which it is applied).

C. Robertson & Co. Ltd.,
71 Park Way,
London NW1.

U.S.A.

Adventure in Crafts Inc.,
218 East 81st Street,
New York, NY 10028.

National Handicraft Co. Inc.,
337 Lincoln Road,
Miami Beach,
FL. 33139.

AUSTRALIA

Craft Plus,
89 Latrobe Terrace,
Paddington 4064.

Melbourne Street Arts & Crafts
Centre,
146 Melbourne Street,
North Adelaide 5006.

NEW ZEALAND

Handicraft House,
37 Orange Avenue,
Penrose,
Auckland.

(All craft supplies. Classes also
conducted.)

Forty Two Handcraft Supplies,
42 Marine Parade,
Paraparaumu,
Wellington.

Index

A
accessories 92
  banana 93
  felt vegetables 92
  fruit 92
  parasol 93
  raffia hat and basket 93–94
armature shapes 55
  wired figures 55

B
bases 30
  nodding head 31
  plastic ball base 31
  weighted tumbling toys 30
bears 10
  Paddington 10
  Pooh 10
  Rupert 10
  Teddy 10
Beatrix Potter 9

C
cheeks 76
circle toys 23
  construction 23–24
claws 85
cleaning toys 104–106
colouring features 77
  acrylic paints 78
  brushes 78
  cold water dyes 78
  emulsion 78
  fabric printing dyes 77
  face powder 77
  food colouring 77
  hot water dyes 78
  indian ink 77
  lipstick 77
  nail polish 77
  oil photographic colours 77
  tea 78
  water colours 78
  wax crayons 77
  wax polish 78
cutting out 19

D
Deans Rag Book Co. 9
design 42
  basic shape 43
  considerations 42

construction of a toy skin 50–52
  darting 48 49
  designing a specific toy subject 59
  designing soft toys 42
  gathering 50
  gussets 46
  inspirational 42
  leg shaping 44
  making toys commercially 135 136
  principles 43
  publishing toy designs 134
  standing toy with four legs 45
development of soft toymaking 8
dolls 8
  boudoir 9
  corset lace 55
  costume 102
  double-ended 129
  French 9
  Jumeau 9
  two-faced reversible 125–127
  walking paper 9
dressing toys 94
  aprons 97
  boater 100
  bodices 95
  bolero 96
  bonnet 99
  cap 99
  designing patterns 94
  dungarees 95
  fastenings 94
  hats 99
  jabot 98
  materials 94
  mob cap 100
  morning coat 96
  nightcap 98
  nightdress 98
  nightshirt 98
  pantaloons 97
  socks 101
  top hat 100
  trimmings 95
  trousers 97
  waistcoat 95 96

E
ears 72
  application 72

  bear 72
  pig 73
  rabbit 73
embroidery in toymaking 102
exhibiting 137
eyebrows 72
eyelashes 71
eyelids 71
eyes
  embroidered 70
  felt 70
  novelty 70
  plastic 69

F
fabrics 13
features 69
feet 84
flat toys, stitch-around method 116
freckles 77

G
Girl's Own paper 9
glove puppets 117
  adding legs 119
  designing 117
  detailed construction 120
  four legs 120
  group project 122
  movable legs 119 120
  music 122
  practice 121
  scenery 122
  stage management 121
glues 13
golliwog 10
  'Mr Smith' 10

H
Hair 79
  applying into a slit 81
  balance 79
  colour 79
  on a band 81
  styling methods 79–81
  wig construction 82

J
Jack-in-the-box 108
  applying lid 111
  dressing subject 109
  fitting spring 109

inserting spring 111
making box 108
securing the lid 111
trimming box 112
Jack-in-the-box puppet 113
jointing 34
combination 37
disc 37
double hinge 34
flange 36
gusset joints 36
lap hinge 35
ne plus ultra 37
parcel hinge 36
pivot hinge 36
shank 37
single hinge 34
socket hinge 35
stitched hinging 34
waist hinge 34
judging 138
comment slips 138
etiquette 138
fur fabric toys 137
knitted toys 138
patchwork toys 138
rag dolls 137

K
Kewpie 10
knitted toys 114
Kruse, Frau Kathe 9
laminating and mask materials 65
designing back of head for a
laminated mask 67
inserting a modelled hand into a
cloth arm 65
laminating a mask — step-by-step
66
laminating material combinations
68
stand to enable easy moulding
of head 64

L
legs 82
rolled felt 84
twisted wool 84

M
manes 85–88
marking out 19
marotte 124
matriochkas 42–43
miniature toys 55
mouths 75
muppets 10
musical units 32

growlers 33
musical box 32
squeakers 33
tinklers 33

N
needle modelling 90
dimples 91
practice head 91
pouties 91
noses 73–74

P
pantin 129–132
paper and card 15
paper mâché 61
hollow head 63
laminated 65
powdered 63
patchwork toys 21
balls 23
hand-sewn 22
machine 22
patterns 16
enlarging and reducing 17–18
rabbit pattern 56
storing 15
templates 16
understanding 16
utilizing a pattern to its fullest
potential 55–58
pinning 20
plaster of Paris 60
plastic wood 61

R
rag dolls
neck gusset 48
neck supports 29
pattern shapes 48
repairing toys 102
old disc jointed bear 103
Roy Lichtenstein 11

S
safety and design 11
British Standards 11
Consumer Protection Regulations
1974 11
European Standards 11
Snoopy 10
snout and beaks 75
Steiff, Fräulein Margarete 9
stitches 24
stitching 20
stuffing 25

T
tails 89
adding a curve 89
adding a tuft 89
techniques, basic 19
teeth 76
tools 12
toy fillings 26–27
beans, lentils, polybeads 27
foam chips 27
foam rubber 27
kapok 26
sawdust and sand 27
synthetic 27

W
whiskers 81 83
wiring 27–29
Wombles 10